USING EXPERIENCE CHARTS WITH CHILDREN

Virgil E. Herrick

Marcella Nerbovig

Charles E. Merrill Publishing Co.
Columbus, Ohio
A Bell and Howell Company

International Standard Book Number: 0-675-09804-1

5 6 7 8 9 10 11 12 13 14 15-76 75 74 73 72 71 70

PRINTED IN THE UNITED STATES OF AMERICA

Preface

The main purpose of this book is to explain and demonstrate the wide use that experience charts have in developing children's understandings and skills in both the language arts and content fields. The experience chart is seen as a concept that may be profitably applied to *all* levels and areas of learning.

The following ideas suggest the broadened perspective from which experience charts can be viewed:

1. The charts are based on some experience that the children and the teacher have had, are having, or are about to have together.
2. The specific subject matter for experience chart writing should be related to an appropriate part of the total experience of the teacher and students together and grow naturally out of that experience and its development.
3. Experience chart writing is based on something children know about, have had an opportunity to observe, explore, try out, and utilize on some first-hand basis.
4. Experience chart writing provides a basis for helping children discover what the real processes of writing are: the alternative ways in which the same idea can be expressed, the ways in which a language choice is resolved, and how improvements can be made in future writing projects.
5. Experience chart writing is a group writing project in which the teacher is an active, responsible participant.
6. Experience chart writing provides a valuable means for enriching and developing language power.
7. Experience chart writing helps a child put the necessary components of writing into their proper relationships and become aware of each necessary contribution.

8. Experience charts may be written to be used many times and for many purposes.

The ideas presented in this book will help teachers use experience charts as an adjunct to other teaching materials or as a substitute for them. The careful presentation of the philosophical basis of experience charts, the detailed description of how to proceed in making charts, and the inclusion of numerous illustrations will enable teachers to begin or extend their use of charts in their teaching of children. The authors not only suggest specific ways to use experience charts, but encourage teachers to find new ways to use charts creatively in their own classrooms. Proper application of the concept of the experience chart insures that teaching materials will be kept up to date, for materials made with and for a given class have a currency that is essential in today's fast changing world.

Many teachers, children, and parents have had a real part in the writing of this book. It is hoped that the expression of their ideas communicates to them the deep appreciation the authors feel.

Photo Credits

The photographs on the following pages are used by courtesy of Wendell H. Pierce, Superintendent of the Cincinnati Public Schools, Cincinnati, Ohio.

Page 14 (top photograph)—From *Focus on Excellence,* Report of the Superintendent, p. 19.

Page 23—From *Seven Significant Years,* Report of the Superintendent, p. 10.

Page 29—From *The Able Learner,* Superintendent's Annual Report, 1957-1958, pp. 4-5.

Page 31—From *Teaching Today,* Report of the Superintendent, p. 10.

Page 45 (top photograph)—From *The Able Learner,* Superintendent's Annual Report, 1957-1958, pp. 16-17.

Page 45 (bottom photograph)—From *Seven Significant Years,* Report of the Superintendent, p. 7.

Page 51—From *Writing: the second R,* Superintendent's Annual Report, p. 23.

Page 68—From *Teaching Today,* Report of the Superintendent, p. 2.

Page 100—From *Seven Significant Years,* Report of the Superintendent, p. 20.

All other photographs are used by courtesy of Northern Illinois University Regional Services, DeKalb, Illinois, Joe Marsh, photographer.

Table of Contents

Chapter One

Important Ideas About Experience Charts

Perhaps you have developed your own notions about what experience charts are and what they can and cannot do in an effective teaching program. Why don't you check your concepts with the following big ideas we have developed as a result of our experiences with them? This may give you a broader perspective on your instructional materials, on how you and your children can create many of them, and on how they can be tied in more intimately with the experience background of children and with your educational objectives.

As you read through this list of ideas, think about them, and perhaps as you study the rest of the book you will think of points in your teaching procedure in which you will want to incorporate some chart development with children; these will be places in which this technique could be most successful and you would be most comfortable.

1. Experience charts are based on some *experience* which the *children and teacher* have had, are having, or are about to have *together.*

   Chart writing may anticipate the experience and thus represent the plans for meeting it; it may be a part of the experience and represent the records to be kept; or chart writing may be a consequence of the experience and thus grow out of it.

2. This experience basis for chart writing varies widely and can provide many different degrees of involvement for both the teacher and children.

   You do not always have to base your experience chart on a formal trip, such as one to the firehouse or zoo. Trips are fine and provide valuable opportunities for many kinds of important learning. But you can also use the many experiences you are having together in your classroom, school, and playground as a basis for writing charts.

   A simple beginning, for example, is deciding on the name of your new hamster and writing his name on a piece of tagboard which you place on the top of his cage to remind you of this decision. Many other activities and events provide similar opportunities for talking, thinking, deciding, and writing. You will find some of these identified and described in the following pages.

3. The specific subject matter for experience chart writing should be related to an appropriate part of the total experience of the teacher and students together and should grow naturally out of that experience.

   As children move into the second and third grades and gain control of the writing skills, you will want to start making decisions about experiences that lend themselves to group development of charts and which are more effective as individual writing projects. In general, the group writing is concerned with those events that are a necessary part of group actions. Individual writing is concerned with the individual extensions of group activities or the unique activities of a single person.

While it is valuable in the initial stages of chart writing with children to have charts tied to simple, unitary experiences such as feeding the fish, the rain outdoors, or the bird on the window sill, there are many more extended activities which are comprehensive enough to permit a number of new charts to grow out of them.

The trip to the firehouse might lead to charts for a list of the things you wish to watch when taking the bus; a description of the fire station; rules about preventing fires; and your reactions to and impressions of the fire truck and Joe the driver.

The important point here is to focus the part of the experience to be used as the subject for writing through discussion and agreement—many times in forms of questions to be answered, things to look for, and results to be planned for. The chart writing is then seen as a natural group responsibility whose form is determined by its purpose.

4. Experience chart writing is based on something children know about, have had an opportunity to observe, explore, try out, and utilize on some first-hand basis.

   Ideas and language grow out of real events and activities. In experience chart writing, the writing is tied to experience and is validated by it.

   Because a child has already seen what he is writing about and has expressed it in a preliminary oral form, he has formed the basis upon which most writing is performed, evaluated, and improved.

5. Experience chart writing provides a basis for helping children discover what the real processes of writing are: the alternative ways in which the same ideas can be expressed, the ways a language choice is resolved, and how improvements can be made in future writing projects.

A child gains experience in verbally "trying on for size" a number of different ways of expressing a given idea. The basis for finally selecting one may be that it seems most appropriate to the subject matter being written upon or most pleasing to him personally.

The child sees writing as an exploratory, tryout process in which he does not expect his writing always to come out just right on the first attempt. He expects to change, improve, and polish his expression and its form as he searches for new and better words, phrases, and language forms to say precisely what he wants to say.

6. Experience chart writing is a group writing project in which the teacher is an active, responsible participant.

After the third grade, the teacher need not always be the writer. Children can assume some of the writing and reading roles. The teacher, however, is always an active facilitating member of the writing group—primarily a helper of the writing process but many times a contributor to the idea as well—when this seems necessary and the teacher can actually make a contribution.

The kind of chart writing we are talking about is really writing by a group of children and their teacher about those things which concern them as a group and need to to be expressed in some form of writing.

A possible special case to this general proposition is when the teacher and a group of children write a story or a poem together as a means for thinking through what this kind of writing means and as a preparation for their own individual creative writing experience. This is no different, actually, from much of the group work done in preparation for individual reading, work in social studies, arithmetic, and science.

Unfortunately, many teachers see chart writing solely as a group preparation for individual writing or for individual learning activities. You will use and develop your chart writing more adequately if you keep the distinction clear.

7. Experience chart writing cannot be adequately defined by any one of the many names given to it.

   Many of the names used for this kind of group writing based on a common experience really express only *one* aspect of this writing, and thus no one name is completely adequate. Actually, all the ideas expressed by these different names when put together give a clear picture of the *multiple* uses of chart writing. Thus:

   Experience Chart emphasizes the experience background for writing.

   Script-Writing underscores the fact that most chart writing uses a manuscript-print form of writing.

   Story Chart emphasizes the story development aspect of group writing and leaves out records of plans, poetic writing, and group letter-writing.

   Classroom Record—frequently called work plan, classroom log, language chart—emphasizes the recording aspects of chart writing, leaving out the other emphases.

   Teacher Chart distinguishes the charts on the basis of who actually writes them. Following this lead there will be *children's charts,* and ultimately Mary's, John's, and Dick's charts.

8. Experience chart writing provides a valuable means for enriching and developing language power.

   The child finds that, by developing his senses and powers of observation, he provides the basis for stretching his thinking and creativeness and thus bringing to life a language power.

   While the content of written or recorded material ought to be significant, one of the major contributions of chart writing with a group of children is its critical and creative attention to the power and function of language itself.

   Since the background ideas and language grow out of real events and activities, they can always be checked and validated by this experience. This process provides a need for new words, new uses for old words, and new language constructions and usage skills.

Because many children are bringing their experience and creative powers to the same writing experiences, enrichment of any single child's language background is bound to take place. There is a broad range of language use; many words and phrases are tried out in a context where every child has an opportunity to tie language symbols to meaningful experiences and to a specific writing purpose.

Chart writing provides a good situation for developing a concern for using the important language tools which the child will continue to use for the rest of his life—the dictionary, thesaurus, encyclopedia, and handbooks of usage and writing format. The child discovers how valuable and necessary such tools are and develops positive attitudes toward their continued use.

9. Experience chart writing helps a child put the necessary components of writing into their proper relationships and become aware of each necessary contribution.

   As every teacher knows, it is frequently difficult for a child to see (a) the importance of study, observation, and use of resources valuable for getting "full of one's subject"; (b) the necessity of thinking through a project to decide what to write about, how it is to be organized and structured, how a particular idea ought to be phrased, and what format and style is most appropriate; and (c) the need for the continuous evaluation and reading necessary to the production of any final writing product.

   In experience chart writing, you do more than talk about the importance of all these aspects—the children and you plunge directly into them as necessary phases, and children are helped to learn how to develop their abilities to deal with them in the future. It is hard to find an effective substitute for this kind of realistic, functional, and constructive learning and teaching.

A second kind of important language relationship is established effectively in experience chart writing. This is the relationship of an experience, with its ideas, structure, and inherent significance, to its manifestation first in oral language, then in written language, and finally in reading what has been written. Thus the child is able to see the valuable and necessary contribution that experience makes to speaking, that speaking makes to writing, and that writing makes to reading. Of course listening is important all through this process.

10. Experience chart writing demands that the teacher have a superior knowledge of the way in which vocabulary development takes place in children and be able to use this knowledge in the writing of experience charts.

    It is well known to every teacher that kindergarten, first, and second grade children are having language experiences that give rise to the need for nouns, adjectives, and verbs (or telling, color, and action words) which give them oral vocabularies different from and sometimes more comprehensive and mature than the reading and writing vocabularies found in their reading and spelling books. Hence, in experience chart writing, since the writing is first framed in the oral speech of children, this preliminary phrasing will contain words and language structure not yet developed in the other areas of the child's language training.

    You should be willing to follow the meaningful oral language of the children, providing you are constantly helping them to deal with it in effective ways.

    It is the thesis of this manual that if you are to help develop a child's language powers to the fullest, you must place the tools for dealing with language effectively into the children's hands as rapidly as possible. This means developing the full range of methods of word attack, an editorial sense for checking writing, and skills in using the dictionary and handbooks for usage. In chart writing you should be demonstrating the use of these skills and materials constantly.

11. Experience chart writing demands that the teacher become skilled in manuscript or cursive writing on the chalkboard and on newsprint before a group.

    Writing with a pen or pencil on ruled paper in the conventional writing position is one thing. Writing with chalk, crayon, or felt pen on unruled chalkboards or newsprint while standing, sitting, or bending over from the side is quite another matter.

    A teacher who is interested in developing chart writing with her children will develop good manuscript and cursive form and then practice it on the chalkboard, newsprint, easels, and work tables. This skill will be useful in chart writing as well as in all your chalkboard work with children.

12. Experience charts may be written to be used many times and for many purposes; they may frequently be revised.

    You will need to have available: newsprint, frames or easels for holding materials for writing, and forms for holding or displaying charts for use.

    It is obvious that chart writing on a chalkboard has many uses but lacks the mobility and permanency necessary for storing and multiple use. Many teachers use the chalkboard for collecting preliminary suggestions for phrasing and then, after examination and selection, transfer the selected phrase or sentence to newsprint. This procedure capitalizes on the ease and flexibility of use of the chalkboard but keeps the advantages of the newsprint and easel.

LET'S CHECK THESE IDEAS AGAIN SO WE CAN KEEP THEM CLEARLY IN MIND!

1. Experience charts are based on some experience which the children and the teacher have had, are having, or are about to have together.
2. The experience basis for chart writing can vary widely and can provide many different forms and purposes for writing

and many different degrees of involvement for both the teacher and children in the writing.

3. The specific subject matter for experience chart writing should be related to an appropriate part of the total experience of the teacher and students together and grow naturally out of that experience and its development.
4. Experience chart writing is based on something children know about, have had an opportunity to observe, explore, try out, and utilize on some first-hand basis.
5. Experience chart writing provides a basis for helping children discover what the real processes of writing are: the alternative ways in which the same idea can be expressed, the ways in which a language choice is resolved, and how improvements can be made in future writing projects.
6. Experience chart writing is a group writing project in which the teacher is an active, responsible participant.
7. Experience chart writing cannot be adequately defined by any one of the many names given to it.
8. Experience chart writing provides a valuable means for enriching and developing language power.
9. Experience chart writing helps a child put the necessary components of writing into their proper relationships and to become aware of each necessary contribution.
10. Experience chart writing demands that the teacher have a superior knowledge of the way in which vocabulary and language development takes place in children in all its aspects and be able to use this knowledge in the writing of experience charts.
11. Experience chart writing demands that the teacher become skilled in manuscript writing on the chalkboard and on newsprint before a group.
12. Experience charts may be written to be used many times, for many purposes, and frequently revised.

Chapter Two

Types of Experience Charts

In thinking about the possible different kinds of experience charts, it might be well to review the following ideas about charts. Experience charts are:

Based on an experience you and your children are having together.

Written by both the teacher and children.

A writing experience whose nature, form, and subject matter are determined by the writing purpose of the on-going group activity and the particular aspect of the experience selected as a focus for the writing.

Read and used by the children and yourself to achieve purposes intended by the group writing experience.

Influenced by the fact that these charts are written records of a social group experience. The identification of leadership responsibilities, the form of the social conventions and values are frequently expressed in the writing (for example, "Thank you, Sharon Lee, for the gift," "We all took a turn calling her," or "Oh! John! You funny boy!") and the personal interactions of group behavior that grow out of the social nature of this writing experience.

As you review the following general categories and specific descriptions of experience charts, keeping the above ideas in mind, you will see how the different illustrations of chart writing are merely combinations of one or a number of the above ideas.

It is convenient to classify different kinds of charts under one of the following categories. Charts are differentiated by:

A. *The purpose for the writing*

Using this referent as a base for distinguishing different kinds of experience chart writing, May Lazar[1] identifies four convenient headings: (1) *Creative Language Charts,* which have as their main purpose the recording of the group's creative language; (2) *Work Charts,* whose main purpose is to organize and facilitate classroom activities; (3) *Narrative Charts,* whose main purpose is to report on or keep a record of some shared experience; and (4) *Reading and Language Skills Charts,* whose main purpose is the teaching and practice of some specific language skill.

B. *The nature of the subject matter*

Surveys of chart practices reveal that charts are used in the development of learning activities in health and safety, reading and the language arts, numbers, sciences, social studies, arts, and in general classroom planning and learning.

As you think about this kind of classification you will realize that it is valuable to help you see all the different areas of the instructional program in which experience chart writing is pos-

---

[1] May Lazar *et al., Experience Charts: A Guide to Their Use in Grades 1-3,* Educational Research Bulletin No. 13, Bureau of Educational Research, Board of Education of the City of New York (May, 1952), p. 3.

sible. It is not equally helpful, however, to suggest the various uses to which charts could be put in dealing with different educational needs in the various subject areas. For example, a narrative chart could be used in health, language arts, reading, science, and social studies. Similarly, charts of reference or rules could be a valuable part of the learning activities of the same subject areas. The same could be true of planning charts. On the other hand, some charts are rather uniquely determined by their subject matter such as phonetic charts, color charts, calendar charts, weather charts, or measures charts.

C. *The use of the chart*

This third way of categorizing or thinking about experience charts emphasizes the functional application of chart writing to educational processes important in all learning. Thus, many teachers think about reference charts, evaluating or testing charts, planning, recording, and informing (naming) charts. In a sense, reading and writing charts derive their names from this same kind of thinking.

It should be clear that this functional classification can be fitted in under each of the subject areas of the previous two headings. Planning, informing, recording, referring, evaluating, as well as reading and writing, are important functions of the learning process in social studies, science, and health, and thus could be effected by appropriate chart writing.

D. *The form of its reproduction*

Of the four ways of identifying and organizing the different kinds of chart writing, this last form is perhaps least significant, although it has certain obvious but rather nondiscriminating values.

Here we find such subclassifications as wall charts; easel charts; primary or intermediate charts; story, diary, or fill-in charts. The charts may also be grouped according to the grade level in which the chart is used or the form in which it is written. Story, diary, and fill-in charts, while consistent with the classification, are different from a wall or script-text chart in that stories and diaries are recognized language forms and suggest many more directives for chart writing than a title such as "wall" chart.

While these four categories help reveal the range and extent of the nature and use of experience chart writing, you will sense that there is no single list of names which will adequately reveal the full extent of the proper use of experience charts. Each of the categories serves to reveal important aspects of experience chart writing, yet no one is sufficient to identify all forms and uses.

As you read this you are probably making the following generalizations:

1. There are many ways to classify and name different kinds of experience charts.
2. The importance of these categories lies in their emphasis on the purpose, function, and area of application of experience charts and not in differences in opinion over the specific names of such categories.
3. The same chart can be used for different purposes, but the name of the category probably need not be changed because of this difference in use.
4. While the kindergarten and first grade will concentrate on naming, narrative, and reading charts because of the level of language development of children, it is likely, if proper adaptations are made, that all forms of charts can be used at all levels.

EXAMPLES OF EXPERIENCE CHARTS

Perhaps the best way to get to the heart of experience chart writing is to study illustrations of the different forms as they are found in the classrooms of many elementary school teachers.

1. Naming Charts

One of the first charts is the name chart that goes above children's lockers, or their tables, or the chalkboard to name the group, etc. This is followed by names for the equipment of the room, pets, work spaces, and the like.

NANCY	SCISSORS
PETER	PAPER
SAM	WATER
	BOOKS

(Each name can be an individual chart.)

2. Picture Charts

A simple form of chart frequently used in lower grades is the picture chart.

The writing here is usually limited to labels or instructional statements about the picture. The pictorial and language symbols are clearly seen by the child as referring to the same experience (object, action, situation).

Pictures can be cut out of magazines, drawn by teachers, or done individually by children.

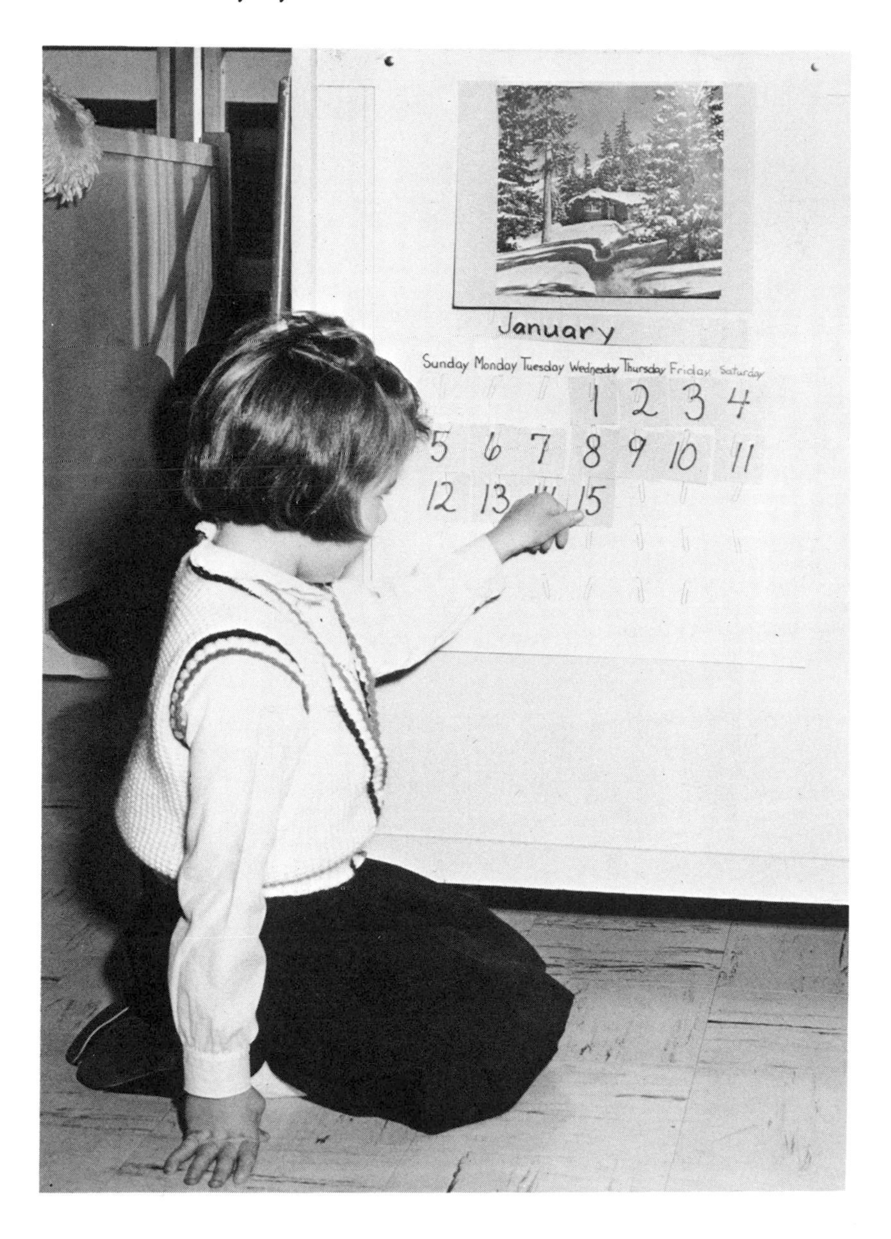

They may be an illustration of a category of things:

Schools
Houses
Birds
People
Tools

They may be a collection of individual charts that illustrate many aspects of a major idea or activity, such as occupations of fathers.

3. Reference Charts

Out of the wide range of activities carried on in the classroom of the individual grades of the elementary school there are many things that need to be recorded and referred to in order to remind, check, indicate the order of activities, and note responsibilities. Reference charts are flexible, convenient, and natural adjuncts to such learning activities. You will find a large part of your chart use falling into this category.

Some of the most common forms of reference charts are the (a) daily duties chart (helpers), (b) calendar and/or weather chart, (c) instructions chart, (d) vocabulary reminder chart, (e) rules chart, (f) informational chart, and (g) summary-plans chart.

a. *Daily Duties Chart.* A natural development of this form of chart is the planning chart for the day's or week's schedule of activities. These are the familiar "Helpers" charts, where the duties remain fairly constant and the names of children change.

Putting the name of each child on tagboard for use on such records saves time.

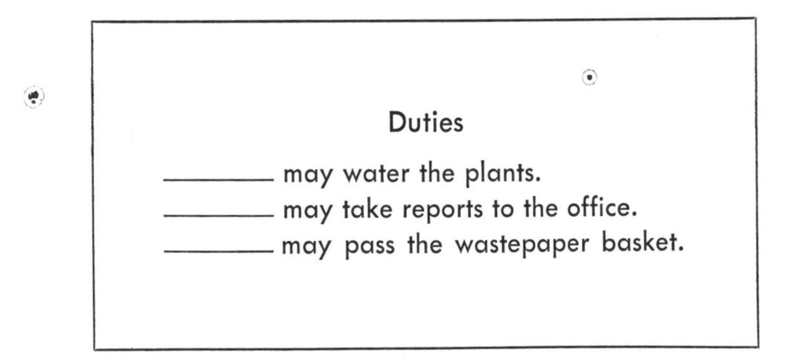

Duties

________ may water the plants.
________ may take reports to the office.
________ may pass the wastepaper basket.

You can sense the many ways in which days of the week and month, assignments to responsibilities, reminders and the like can be the basis for a chart reference and use.

Plans for the Week

Monday we go to the gym.
Tuesday we go to the library.
Wednesday we listen to 'Let's Draw.'
Thursday Miss Smith comes in for art.
We bring milk money on Friday.

Birthdays this week: ________
____
____

Library Groups

Monday	Wednesday
Deborah	Erick
Seymour	Kristin
Lynn	Gregory
Susan	Seth
Julie	Martha

Some teachers use a fixed time schedule—others vary for different days of the week, others utilize blocks of time within which plans are developed. As larger blocks of time are used there is greater need for planning and scheduling within them and planning charts are very useful.

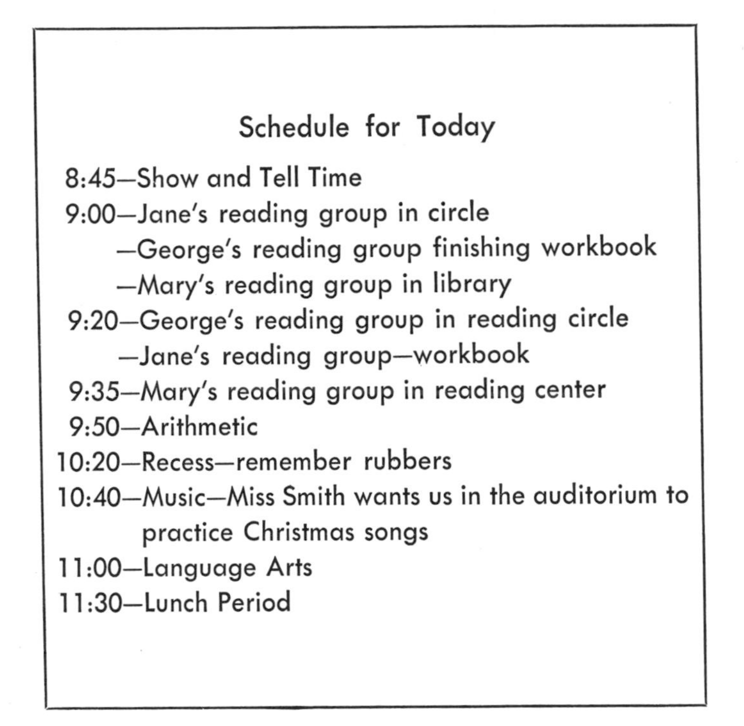

Schedule for Today

8:45—Show and Tell Time
9:00—Jane's reading group in circle
—George's reading group finishing workbook
—Mary's reading group in library
9:20—George's reading group in reading circle
—Jane's reading group—workbook
9:35—Mary's reading group in reading center
9:50—Arithmetic
10:20—Recess—remember rubbers
10:40—Music—Miss Smith wants us in the auditorium to practice Christmas songs
11:00—Language Arts
11:30—Lunch Period

b. *Calendar and/or Weather Chart.* Common forms are:
Day of the week chart
Marking off the days of the month chart

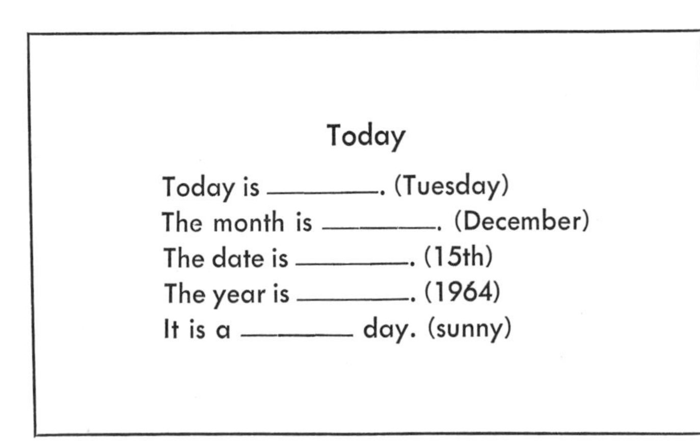

Today

Today is ________. (Tuesday)
The month is ________. (December)
The date is ________. (15th)
The year is ________. (1964)
It is a ________ day. (sunny)

c. *Instructions Chart.* All kinds of construction projects and "do it yourself" aspects of the classroom and school living provide opportunities for effective chart development and use. A common form is the chart of instructions for use of equipment, materials, or for procedure.

Feeding the Fish

FOOD package is on the tank shelf.
Shake a little on top of water.
DON'T use too much.
Put package back.
Work quietly.
Feed only once a day.

Many teachers have difficulty in organizing the storage of materials and use of equipment in the room. Labels, list charts, and agreements on where things will be kept go a long way to create a well-organized, smooth-running room.

Materials in This Drawer

Drawing Paper	Writing Paper
Blue	½″ spaces
Orange	(big)
Red	
Black	
Yellow	½″ spaces
White	(small)

Instructions for using common school facilities may call for reminders of familiar signs. These signs control leaving the room, going to washroom, etc.

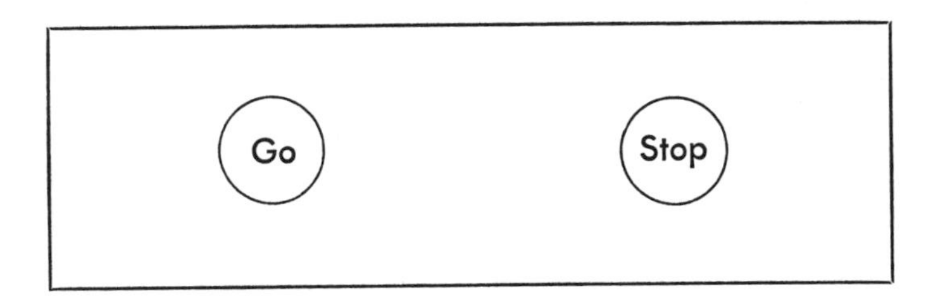

The recipe chart makes instructions accessible to all.

How to Make a Mask

Here is some paper.
Use your scissors.
Cut holes for eyes, nose, mouth.
Color the face you want.
Use string to tie it on.

d. *Vocabulary Reminder Chart.* The reminder chart, the instruction, and the rules chart are very much alike. The difference between these reference charts is (1) instruction charts tell how some process or act is carried on, (2) reminder charts are really notes to ourselves telling us to remember to do something we originally planned to do, and (3) rules charts are principles of action, criteria for judging, or charters for action.

INSTRUCTION CHART

REMINDER CHART

Think

Read the problem carefully!
What information is given?
What do you want to find?
Will your plan give you the answer?
How will you check your answer?
Have you written your solution neatly?

REMINDER CHART

For Tomorrow

We are taking our trip to the zoo.
Remember to bring the permission note from your parent.
Be sure you know the plans for the trip.
You may bring your camera.

REMINDER CHART

Before Going Home:

pick up paper.
put things away.
sit quietly.

REMINDER CHART

We Still Need:

two candles.
one package of napkins.
three cakes.
one storyteller.

RULES CHART

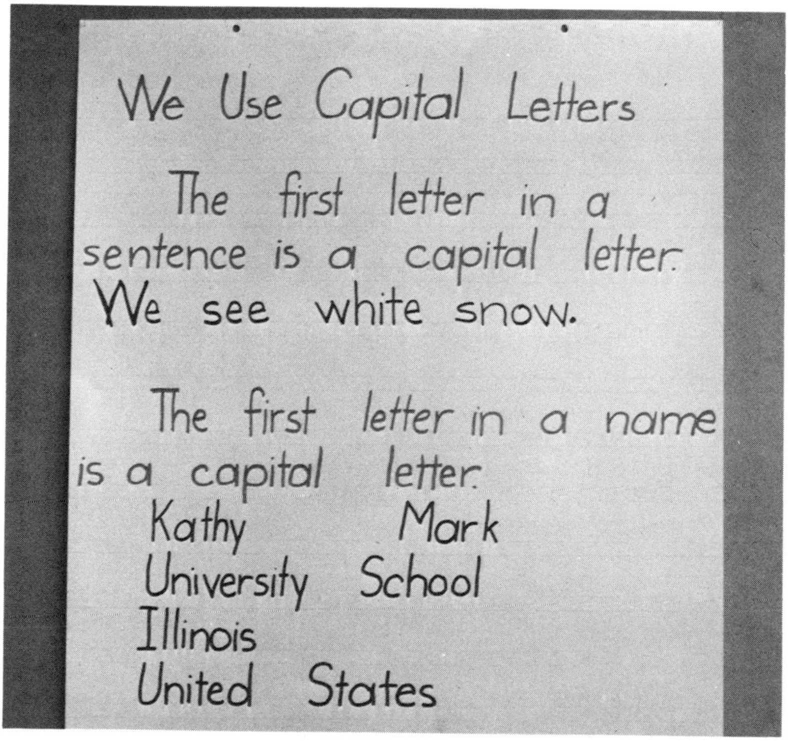

We Use Capital Letters

The first letter in a sentence is a capital letter.
We see white snow.

The first letter in a name is a capital letter.
Kathy Mark
University School
Illinois
United States

e. *Rules Charts.* We have discussed the rules charts briefly. These are the familiar charts developed with a class as rules, agreements, and criteria for action and behavior.

How to Care for a Book

1. Have clean hands.
2. Keep books off the floor.
3. Do not tear the pages.
4. Hold books properly.
5. Never write in books.

SANITATION

I. PROTECT YOUR CLOTHES WITH AN APRON.

II. WASH HANDS THOROUGHLY WITH SOAP.

III. HAVE A DAMP CLOTH READY TO WIPE UP SPILLS.

IV. NEVER COMB HAIR WHILE PREPARING FOOD.

V. TIE LONG HAIR BACK.

VI. KEEP FINGERS AWAY FROM HAIR, MOUTH, AND FACE.

VII. REPLACE ALL ITEMS AS SOON AS YOU HAVE MEASURED OUT THE MATERIALS YOU NEED.

VIII. KEEP A DISH NEAR THE STOVE FOR DIRTY UTENSILS.

These charts may vary widely in their usefulness depending on how closely they really represent the understanding and value convictions of the group of children developing them. They are most valuable when they truly represent the common agreements of the class for directing behavior.

Things We Will Try to Do

Make sure we know what we are to do.
Make sure we do it as well as we can.

Charts such as these worked out with children and then used

will save many hundreds of admonitions, scoldings, and criticisms by the teacher.

Crossing the Street

1. Watch traffic lights.
2. Watch the walk signs.
3. Obey helpers like school patrol or policeman.
4. Look both ways—first to left, then to right.

These charts, appropriately keyed to the language and concerns of a given group of children, can be used at every grade level of the elementary school.

Using Slides

Wait until person is off before you slide down.
Get out of the way when you reach the bottom.
Sit down and face forward when sliding down.

Swings

One person in a swing at a time.
Sit down when swinging.
The swing goes forward and backward, not sideways.
Stay away from swings in motion.

The following rule chart is familiar to every first grade teacher.

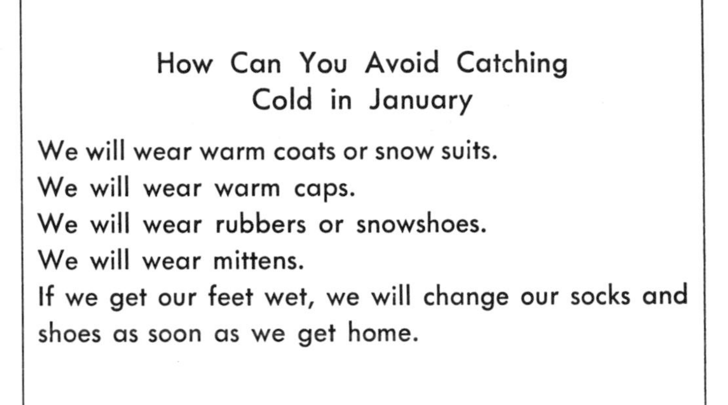

How Can You Avoid Catching
Cold in January

We will wear warm coats or snow suits.
We will wear warm caps.
We will wear rubbers or snowshoes.
We will wear mittens.
If we get our feet wet, we will change our socks and shoes as soon as we get home.

Here is a chart developed from agreements made for the walk to the duck pond.

Safety During Our Walk

1. Stay in groups
2. Keep in line
3. Listen to directions
4. Keep moving with the line

f. *Information Chart.* The purpose of this chart is to record the information the class group needs for its project or future learning activities.

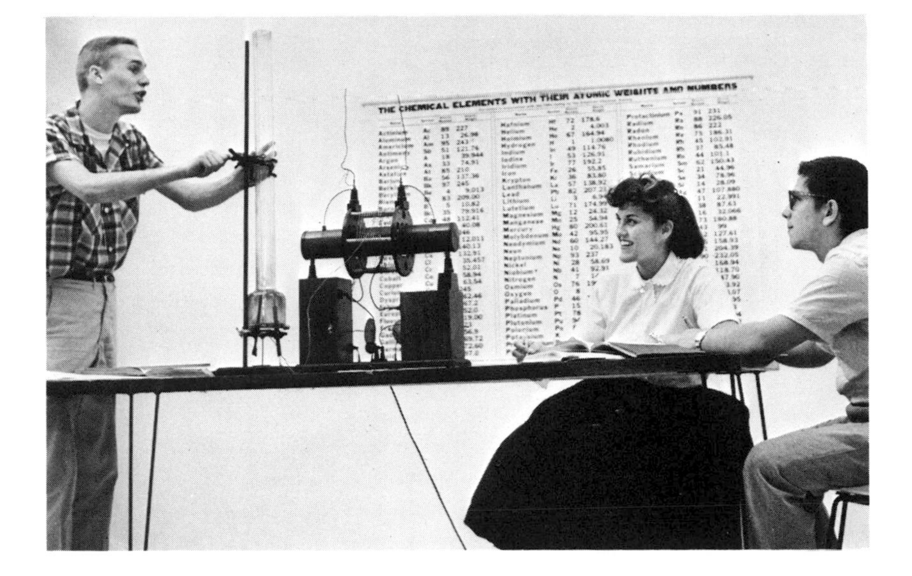

Magnets

Magnets are of different sizes.
Magnets are of different shapes.
Magnets are of different colors.
Magnets attract some things.
Magnets do not attract some things.
Magnets attract these things in our room:

- paper clips
- scissors
- nails
- pins
- cover on paste jar

Some teachers reserve the name "experience chart" for this kind of writing because it is frequently a simple, straightforward account of some experience.

Boats

Boats are made to carry people and materials on water. They act like cars and trucks do on roads. Or like airplanes do in air.

Boats can carry people for fun or as a business. George, Francine, and Erick and their families rode on a car ferry across Lake Michigan this summer. This boat carried both cars and people. Their parents paid a fee for each car and person.

There are many kinds of boats, of different sizes and pushed by different kinds of power—oars and your muscles, sails, outboard motors, inboard motors, steam engines, and large turbines or electric motors.

Many of our families own small boats. Some of us have traveled on large ocean liners to Europe and to Japan. We enjoyed riding on the elevators, playing on deck, and swimming in the swimming pools.

Do you know how these large boats find their way across the ocean?

There are many opportunities during social studies, science, arithmetic, etc., to summarize the major points learned.

There are two types of plants

A. Those without seeds—spore flowers
B. Those with seeds
   1. Some seeds are grown in flowers
      fruits
      beans
      peas
   2. Some seeds are grown in cones
      pine
      spruce
      hemlock
      fir

Many teachers develop this kind of chart for collecting information around topics being studied. This chart can be used in all subject areas and at all levels.

There is an important relationship between this kind of group writing and the individual writing of each student as he works on his reports, notes, and stories.

It is likely that a teacher should maximize the practice in decision-making involved in this kind of writing so each child is better able to do this for himself: what things should be said, how do we choose, and how should we say them—in what order and in what paragraph structure. Every child needs help on these questions in writing.

Many teachers use this chart as a reading chart—frequently called a narrative chart.

Birds

Many birds are seen on the farms. Robins, bluebirds, bluejays, pheasants, cardinals, and quails are to be seen.

In making these charts, it is obvious you will want to make sure the necessary research and study have been done to assure the authenticity of the information being written. You will also want to help children verify the things they write by checking the sources as they develop the chart.

Here, also, the format, length of sentences, paragraphing, structure of sentence and language units become important and should be discussed.

Dear Dr. Herrick,

We had fun at your handwriting class. We would like to do it again and again. We have been studying the sky. Craig Harris has a coin collection.

Karen has a stone collection.

We were on television.

We want you to come again.

Your friends,

Miss Smith's Class
Midvale School

Another kind of informational chart writing consists of what some teachers call class logs or diary writing. This is keeping a group record of how a project develops with the necessary reference material or merely a straightforward recording of each day. It is frequently combined with time in the daily program for reviewing, summarizing, or evaluating. Here *time* is a common referent for structuring the chart.

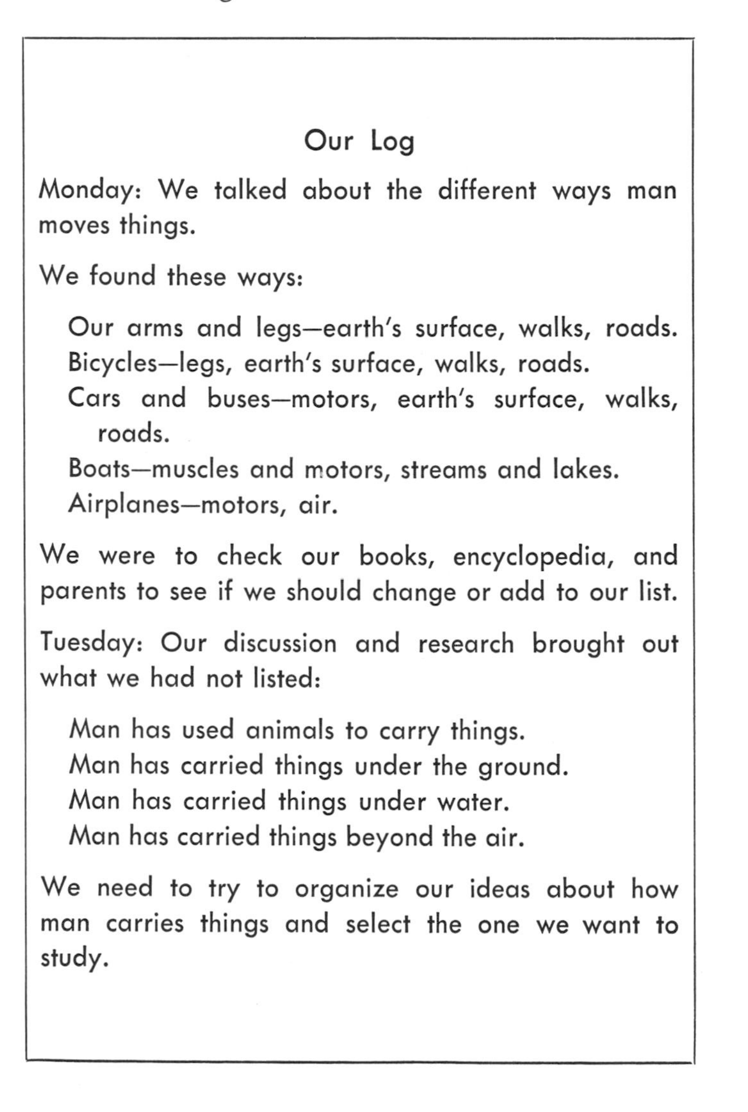

Our Log

Monday: We talked about the different ways man moves things.

We found these ways:

Our arms and legs—earth's surface, walks, roads.
Bicycles—legs, earth's surface, walks, roads.
Cars and buses—motors, earth's surface, walks, roads.
Boats—muscles and motors, streams and lakes.
Airplanes—motors, air.

We were to check our books, encyclopedia, and parents to see if we should change or add to our list.

Tuesday: Our discussion and research brought out what we had not listed:

Man has used animals to carry things.
Man has carried things under the ground.
Man has carried things under water.
Man has carried things beyond the air.

We need to try to organize our ideas about how man carries things and select the one we want to study.

Some teachers use this kind of chart to record observations of such activities as the mother hen and hatching of chickens, watching frog eggs change to tadpoles, a seed sprouting, the changes on a gelatin culture, etc.

May 1. Today Mary brought six eggs. We put them into the nest. Our hen is sitting on them.
May 5. Still sitting!
Some dads say the hen is setting.
May 12. No chickens yet!
May 17. Some eggs are cracking.
May 18. Four tiny chickens.
Two did not hatch.
Their feathers are like soft fur.
Nov. 16. Snowed today. We saw a picture on sunfish with Mr. Jones' room.
Nov. 17. Talked over our plans for Thanksgiving program. We are to be Indians and will do a Thanksgiving dance. Miss Jelnick's room will be Pilgrims.
Nov. 18. Took a trip to the Arboretum.

The regular diary of each day or of a week's happenings is really a summary of the total happenings of the period and contains many unrelated things. Such charts lack the focus and specificity of the other illustrations given here.

g. *Summary-plans Charts.* It is clear that many of the previously described charts contain an important planning dimension. It should be realized that one important planning chart is the one which collects for future reference the questions, problems, and things to be looked for for subsequent learning activities, such as the information chart.

Things We Want to Know About Air

1. We cannot see it, smell it, or taste it. How can we observe it? Measure it? Control it?
2. Does air occupy space? We talk about compressed air—what does this mean? How can air be pushed together?
3. We learned that boats use sails to move on the water and that airplanes move in the air. We said that air pushes the boats; does air push the airplane?
4. We learned that we and other animals cannot live without air. We watched a candle go out when a glass jar was put over it. What does air give us so we can live and the candle burn?

You will expect to come back to this chart to verify, eliminate, and add to it as you and your group see more clearly what you wish to do and accomplish.

It should be clear to you that this chart is unfinished and will be added to, that the teacher is asking questions with the children, and that unless this list of questions is used for future planning and evaluation, you cannot justify the time spent. If used, this chart can be very effective.

As you work with your children in chart development you will find new forms to add to the list.

You will find many uses and places for such chart development. You will also sense an important relationship between group development of these general charts and their use and application to activity by individual children. Their availability and durability characteristics are important considerations in insuring this use.

4. Evaluation Charts

This kind of chart can be used to review, to summarize, and to evaluate.

Some teachers use the picture chart with questions.

Children can use this chart to compare their own manuscript letter forms.

Some teachers make their own writing scale by gathering writing samples from a group and arranging them in order of legibility.

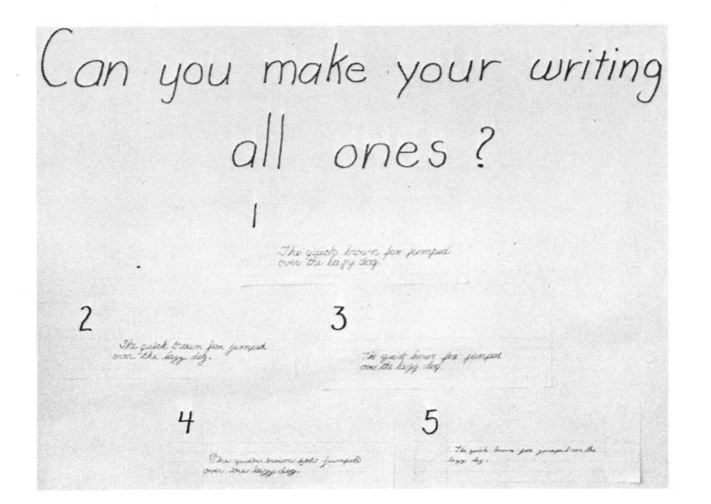

A multiple choice chart can be used.

Pick Out the Right Answers

1. Which one is a grain?	cherries potatoes soy beans
2. Which one gives us milk?	mule goat chicken
3. Which ones give us feathers?	sheep ducks dogs
4. Which one is a fruit?	orange carrots cabbage

Every reading teacher has used the "Guess Who?" or "What Am I?" charts. The children enjoy making them. Many times after the class has made one or two, individual children add many more to the "Who Am I?" booklet of charts.

Who Am I?

I run down the street.
I bounce and jump and wag my tail.
I love to chase balls and cats.
When I'm happy I bark.
I am a ________.

5. Creative Writing Charts

Creative writing is seen by many teachers as a personal individual act—not a group enterprise. Thus they do not place high importance on group creative writing of charts in their classroom activities.

There is a place, however, for the group writing of creative charts.

All story charts have a high element of creativity.

A group of children and their teacher can write just as creatively in both prose and poetic form about the things which interest them as can individuals.

The group writing experience with its wide range of suggestions for expression is frequently a sound base for encouraging and enriching individual creative writing.

There is no competition or conflict between group and individual creative writing. Each complements the other.

A rural school teacher concerned about the stilted writing of her children in her eight grade, twenty-pupil school suggested one October afternoon that they all go out in the schoolyard and try to sense what they wanted to say about the schoolyard, the fields, the hills, the sky and sun, and the dusty roads. After spending 15-20 minutes making mental and written notes they returned to share their contributions in a common chart.

An October Afternoon

Teacher and Children:	Our schoolhouse sits gathering its shadows and children around it.
Mac (1st grade):	The sun is going down. I'm going home.
Mary (3rd grade):	I could rest in the blue of the sky.
Sue (3rd grade):	The hills send out shadows like fingers to catch the day.
George (6th grade):	A car pulls its kite of dust behind it.
Pete (7th grade):	My paper and pencil stop my tongue. It is nice to sit in the warm sun.

A second grade teacher with her children on a play-yard when it was snowing came in to write:

Snow, Snow, Snow

Quiet as my pussycat.
Soft as my mother's cheek.
A star on my coat sleeve.
Wet as the sidewalk.
Cool on my fingers.
Snow, Snow, Snow.

Commonly Used Forms for Creative Writing Charts.

a. The descriptive statement chart about a common experience. Remember:

   1. Grade level does not always determine the quality of the contribution.
   2. You will want to avoid getting into writing "ruts." Be quick to catch and encourage new directions, aspects to be sensed, and phrasing to be cherished!
   3. Chart writing does not have always to be deliberately functional and carefully structured.

b. The story to be read from a series of charts.

1st Chart:	The bell went clang! clang! The whistle went whooo!
2nd Chart:	Here comes the firetruck. Here come the firemen.
3rd Chart:	Up, up, the ladder they go. In, in, the door they go.
4th Chart:	The smoke stops. The fire is out.
5th Chart:	The bell goes clang! clang! Away they go!

The children can sense the structure and development of a story. Many times their directness and parsimonious writing is worthy of emulation by adults.

c. Some teachers feel that creative chart writing should be like the writing in many primers and first readers used in the reading class.

Sally Sees Santa

Run, Dick and Jane.
Come and see Santa.
See the sleigh.
See all Santa's reindeer.
Oh! Oh! Oh!

A Dog for Dick

Come here, Sally.
Come here, Jane.
Come here, George.
See my dog.
His name is Spot.

We feel that these examples of such writing should not be copied. That would make chart writing a dry, dreary, and monotonous activity. Yet you may find this kind of chart writing valuable as a reading chart used to supplement the basic reading materials.

d. Narrative or informational charts can have their creative phrasing. Following is a chart dictated by kindergarten children. Until teachers observe such charts being written, they do not realize that kindergarten children can talk this way with this level vocabulary.

Dinosaurs

This fossil is like a thunder lizard.
The king of the tyrants is a meat eater.
The duckbill can swim.
The terrible fish can eat other fish.
When dinosaurs get big, they could almost reach the cloud.

e. Don't forget the poetic form! Children can sense rhythm and the sound of the things they want to say.

Winter is fun,
With its ice and snow,
We slide and we run,
And we shout "Ho, ho!"

A Valentine

This heart is pretty
As you can see.
It goes to you
And comes from me.

I know a little flower
That just had a shower.

Tops spin.
Round and round they go—
Fast, fast, fast.
Slow, slow, slow.
Wobble, wobble.
Tumble.
Stop.

Since poems are written to be read, chart writing with its oral phrasing, writing, and then reading is an excellent vehicle.

6. Vocabulary and Language Charts

Collections of words you use to form phonetic generalizations.

The Sounds of "ed"

ed as ed	ed as t	ed as d
planted	helped	lived
shouted	jumped	played
skated	liked	waved
wanted	looked	pulled

Various meanings of a word.

Scale

I can scale the mountain.
I can play a scale on the piano.
I can scale a fish.
I can weigh myself on a scale.

A collection of words growing out of a unit. Foreign words or phrases.

Spanish

Senor	—	Mr.
Senora	—	Mrs.
Senorita	—	Miss
si	—	yes
dodo	—	sleepyhead
toro	—	bull
gato	—	cat

Cumulative Lists. Animals we have seen this month.

Animals

Robins	Turtles
Bluebirds	Pigs
Pheasants	Squirrels
Crows	Rabbits
Cardinals	Deer
Ducks	Gophers
Geese	

People who come to our house.

Antonyms.

These charts may serve as reference charts, as summary charts, and as evaluation charts. It is clear that these charts are somewhat different from the creative writing charts just illustrated.

The illustrations given in this section can be extended in many ways. They should, however, give you some sense of the wide array of activities which can involve chart writing.

Chapter Three

Planning and Developing Experience Charts

In making and using experience charts, there are three distinct, accumulative activities. A teacher and a group of children will have an experience in common, they will talk about the experience and write it down, and the children will, with guidance, read the recorded experience. Each of these activities is important in its own right and each an essential part of the total activity. You cannot take for granted the breadth or depth of children's experiences, their ability to phrase and organize ideas, or their ability to read what they themselves have dictated.

This chapter will take each of these phases of chart making and discuss it in detail.

THE EXPERIENCE

A child reads with interest and vitality materials which are written from experiences he has had and has shared with his class. The experience is more appropriate for chart use if it provides a variety of concepts and vocabulary. These concepts and words should be related to a unifying topic.

KINDS OF EXPERIENCES

Experiences for chart making can grow out of classroom or out-of-school interests of children.

A picture contributed by you or a child, cut and mounted, can serve as the beginning of a chart.

Classroom interest centers such as the science area—experiments with iron filings and a magnet, bread mold and a microscope, or experiences with a hen and chicks—may serve as another.

Dramatic play situations related to a story or unit in progress —a market day in the Orient, work our fathers do, the driving of the golden spike—serve as energizers of written expression.

The experience for the chart writing may be an excursion into the community outside the school such as a trip to a farm, a day in court, or a visit to some historic shrine.

You and the children may capitalize on the ordinary things to be seen by children on their way from home to school. Frequently and effectively used centers of attention are observations of nature such as birds or signs of spring or vehicles such as bicycles, wagons, and airplanes. Appeals to other senses such as sound or smell can be used: the sound of a train in the distance, church chimes, or birds; the smell of flowers, a bakery, or burning leaves.

Experiences that are real, pictured, or played, that are elaborate or homely, can be used as the first step in reading from creative writing.

Not All Experiences Need Be Used for Charts

It is neither desirable nor possible that you give full use to every experience by discussing and recording it. Charts, when overused, can lose their interest and value as easily as any other technique of teaching.

You will know from the reactions of the children which experience will hold their interest. You gain this insight from your study and knowledge of children in general and from close study and observation of your group of children. A group of twenty-five or more children will give evidence of a great variety of interests.

Important as children's interests are, this vast number of interests demands that you do some selecting from among them. To do this well, you will keep in mind the real and lasting value for children of this topic as a center of attention. Current events which are transitory or sensational need careful scrutiny. For example, a kidnapping might be of great current interest to children: this does not make it a good topic for an experience chart. Items that fall in the realm of sensational, morbid, or the unlawful have little place in the materials and ideas for classroom instruction. Many times, however, you will find it desirable to focus on safety behaviors that would help children to avoid similar unfortunate incidents.

Safe Operation Procedure

1. Blade projects ⅛″ to ¼″ above work
2. Stand to one side of work—not behind it
3. Use push stick when sawing small pieces
4. Be sure guard is on saw
5. Use miter gauge for cross cutting
6. Use rip fence for ripping
7. Roll sleeves above elbows
8. Pay attention to your work!!

DISCUSSING THE EXPERIENCE

Following the actual experience, but preceding the writing and reading of the record, considerable discussion and thought are engaged in concerning the nature and organization of the things that might be written. This discussion and consideration serves a number of purposes. First, each child has an opportunity to contribute to the fund of information being built for possible use in the writing and to gain practice in expressing himself. Next, when concepts and misconceptions or partial ideas held by children are stated, they can be verified, reinforced, corrected, or expanded. Third, there is an opportunity for you to assess what the children have learned in order to plan more realistically for the next steps in developing needed concepts and skills and for organizing their learnings into an appropriate sequence for writing. Finally, the basis is laid for a pattern of thinking and action important in the future writing activities of each child.

The Child	*The Teacher*
Thinks	Listens
Discusses	Corrects
Contributes	Accepts
Dictates	Verifies
Listens	Adds
Compares	Questions
Considers	Records
Arranges	Guides
Records	Assesses
Corrects	Plans

Emphasis here is on rounding out, clarifying, and trying the ideas rather than simply trying to verbalize the action.

RECORDING AND WRITING

During the discussion, notes concerning the major ideas expressed by children are made. If you are a teacher of young children, you will need to act as recorder; in the intermediate grades children may take notes for use in the future actual writing. When notes and the tapering off of productive discussion indicate that the ideas have been well explored, the formal written record of the material is made. You can initiate this by asking, "How shall we say this so that others may read about it, too?" This is followed by a period of roughing out what is going to be said, to whom, and for what purpose.

Statements of the ideas are volunteered by children and recorded where all can read them. Several children may offer what each conceives to be the optimum expression of a given idea. Each idea should be judged on its own merits and worked through by the class until consensus is reached as to its significance for inclusion and suitability of expression.

During the writing of this chart the teacher emphasized the following vocabulary: stick, point, players, hit, and hitters. Special attention was drawn to the similar endings of "players" and "hitters" in the completed chart.

You will want to think about how to write the ideas down in phrases and sentences. Many times the statement is incomplete and you may wonder if you should put it into a complete sentence form or just write it as the child states it. Teachers differ in the extent to which they rewrite or restate what the children have said. In general, it is better to begin with children's phrasing and then help them rewrite into adequate form. For example, "Chickens do not," was rewritten to say: "Chickens do not fly." (Some children challenged this, saying they had seen chickens fly.) The final phrasing was: "Chickens do not fly in the way wild ducks do."

When the ideas are rephrased, if necessary, they are put into the desired sequence. Children inexperienced in organizing ideas may require teacher guidance in the form of leading questions. The teacher may ask, "What happened first?" "How did it look?"

News

Today is Monday, December 14, 1964. It is windy and sunny. Today our class has art. Our student teachers are here today. They watch us work and help us.

Features of this chart include:

1. review of the placement of the comma in a date,
2. discussion and decision regarding the tense of the verb in line 3,
3. discussion and decision about exactness of expression in line 3 when "are" was chosen over "arrived," and the addition of "help us." The decision was based on the criterion that the chart should "really tell something,"
4. that it would be added to later in the day.

You might be able to write the final form of the chart quickly and neatly so that the finished chart may be produced and used immediately. If you are less skilled in writing, however, you could engage the class in another activity; this would give you an opportunity to make the final copy of the chart at a later time. It is also possible that a child or a group of children can make the final copy.

THE TITLE

In some instances the total chart will be recorded, then the title is developed as a generalization.

In other cases, the chart will be developed from the title. That is, the major idea will be presented first, then the remainder of the narrative will be developed deductively.

Young children tend to think of the title additively. When a title is called for, the child is likely to respond by stringing together all the ideas; a very long title may result. Knowing this, you can help children by asking them to think of "two or three words" that tell the "main idea" in the chart. Since generalizing is an important skill in both language and thinking, its development should be maximized.

The Hungry Cat

Tabby ran to the store.
He said, "Meow."
Mr. Brown gave milk to Tabby.
Tabby said, "Mew, mew."

ILLUSTRATIONS

As in the case of the title, illustrations may furnish the impetus for the chart story itself, or may come as the finishing touch on a chart.

Unlike the title, however, illustrations for a chart may be eliminated. If used, illustrations serve to supplement or emphasize concepts expressed in the verbal portion of the chart.

Illustrations also help to make charts attractive. Pictures that illustrate key or obscure concepts may be selected or drawn either by you or by children. Occasionally clues to difficult words or ideas can be given in the text of a chart by the use of rebus—substituting a picture for a word.

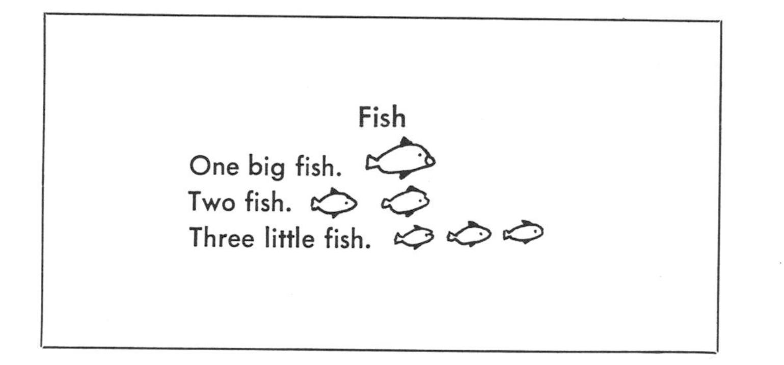

THE USE OF THE CHART

During the recording of the chart, children read each sentence silently or semi-audibly as it is being recorded and aloud as soon as recording is completed. Beginning readers may read the entire completed chart orally in unison. Older children will read the entire chart or portions of it individually.

Rereading continues until the ideas and their expression are recalled easily by the children, but not to the point of boredom.

At the completion of the recording of ideas, the chart is reread by the teacher or by a class member who reads fluently. Corrections are made of any inconsistencies that are apparent in the accuracy of ideas, in the expression of ideas, or in their sequential placement.

Subsequent uses of the chart, during a different period on the same day or on following days, will depend on the reason for the material having been recorded, the challenge this chart offers for these particular children, and the possibilities the ideas and vocabulary hold for continued and varied use.

Not all charts need to be used for formal instruction in reading skills and vocabulary. However, to be useful for any of the purposes described in Chapter 2, the steps described above will need to be observed. It is well for you to be aware, however, that no instructional material can do everything. One kind of material frequently enriches the use of every other appropriate material. You will see the values of different kinds of materials for the achievement of the various objectives of teaching and learning. You will want to use charts for what they can do best in the same manner as prepared materials are used for what they can do. Charts used to precede, enrich, and extend other materials make a real contribution to the learning of children.

TIME

How much time does all this involve? Time and the use of charts can be looked at in two ways. First, how much of the above should you try to accomplish in a given period? Second, for how many days or weeks or months should a given chart be used?

Again you will have to look at the task and at the children before the first question can be answered. If a major excursion is taken, its duration will limit the amount of time that can be spent on follow-up activities on any given day. Therefore, a general discussion might be held, postponing the formal discussion, organization, and recording until the next day. Use of the chart for reading or reference might take place on the third day.

On the other hand, a particular experience, though brief, might be of sufficient impact to carry your class through the total operation in one period, with frequent returns to the chart to keep the experience fresh. The magnitude of the task and the ability of the children to sustain interest would serve as criteria for you in making decisions about how long a period to spend on a given chart experience. Repeated use of a chart would depend on the interest of the children and your ability to provide varied and worthwhile activities with it. Generally, a new chart is preferred to overuse of an old one. Of course charts of rules, standards of behavior, or questions to be answered in a unit would be available for reference all through the unit or throughout the year.

SUMMARY

An experience chart is a vehicle for teaching and learning attitudes, skills, and concepts. It has intrinsic value to children when it is a valued record of something that needed recording. The ideas and their expression are fused into the chart, a tangible evidence of an important learning experience.

The following references describe how others have proceeded in experience chart use.

Chappel, B. M. "Are You Using Pupil-Made Charts?" *Grade Teacher,* 73:48 (April, 1956).

A brief, personal account of uses and construction of experience charts.

Liechti, A. O., and Chappell, J. R. *Making and Using Charts.* (San Francisco: Fearon Publishers, 1957, 1960).

Directions, materials, and a variety of well-illustrated chart suggestions are offered.

Rothschild, A. E. "Charts, and How to Use Them," *Grade Teacher,* 72:59 (October, 1954).

A delightfully written overview of the advantages in using charts, and an episode describing the making of a chart plus sample charts of cooperatively written poems.

Chapter Four

Charts for Reading

Learning to read is dependent upon a number of factors, which can be classified under two headings relating to the child: his experience and his maturation. The wide range of individual differences in relation to these factors found among children in any schoolroom is well known to teachers. Differences among children in interests and abilities make it necessary for a teacher to make some curricular provision. Often this is a real challenge. One of the ways you might deal with this problem is to use, in greater or lesser degree, materials which you make for children or develop cooperatively with the children. These teacher-made or teacher-child-made materials are useful in "real reading" [1] instruction as well as instruction at the readiness level of normal children, or instruction of exceptional children.

---

[1] Gertrude Hildreth, *Teaching Reading* (New York: Holt, Rinehart & Winston, Inc., 1958), p. 222.

READINESS

It is generally agreed that there is little place for charts or reading in the ordinary sense in nursery school, although signs and name tags are used as labels, as for example on their "cubbies" or lockers. Checklists of skills may be used in nursery school or kindergarten.

Here are some ways reading charts can help develop reading readiness in kindergarten and first grade children.

1. Help build vocabulary. Expand the speaking and hearing vocabulary as well as later developing reading or sight vocabulary.

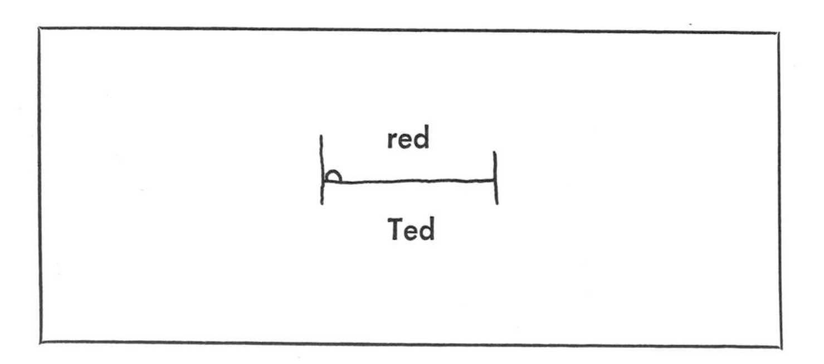

sometimes
someone
someday

2. Help establish and clarify the relationship between writing and reading. Children will see that meaning can be secured from print.

3. Help in using language units. Phrases and sentences are the units in which ideas are expressed; words are the unit of pronunciation. Reading grows from the children's spoken words to written phrases and sentences and stories.

4. Help express ideas in logical sequence.

> The man stopped the car.
> He got out of the car.
> Then he walked to the house.

5. Help develop respect for the written words and pride in self-authorship.

6. Help in beginning the development of mechanical skills involved in reading, i.e., focusing eyes on print; the conventions of reading from left to right, the return sweep, and from top-to-bottom of the page progression.

7. Help children develop the study skills of paying attention, keeping the place, and seeing differences in language symbols and forms.

> Leaves
>
> Red leaves.
> Green leaves.
> Yellow leaves.

8. Help children learn to focus attention. The large size of a chart permits easier and clearer demonstration by the teacher in class instruction when attention needs to be called to particular points concerning the reading. Close observation of your children when writing and using charts together gives you an opportunity to identify the areas in

which special reading help will be needed by children. The size of the chart also permits a child to react with an arm or his whole body, an important possibility for children who derive joy from movement.

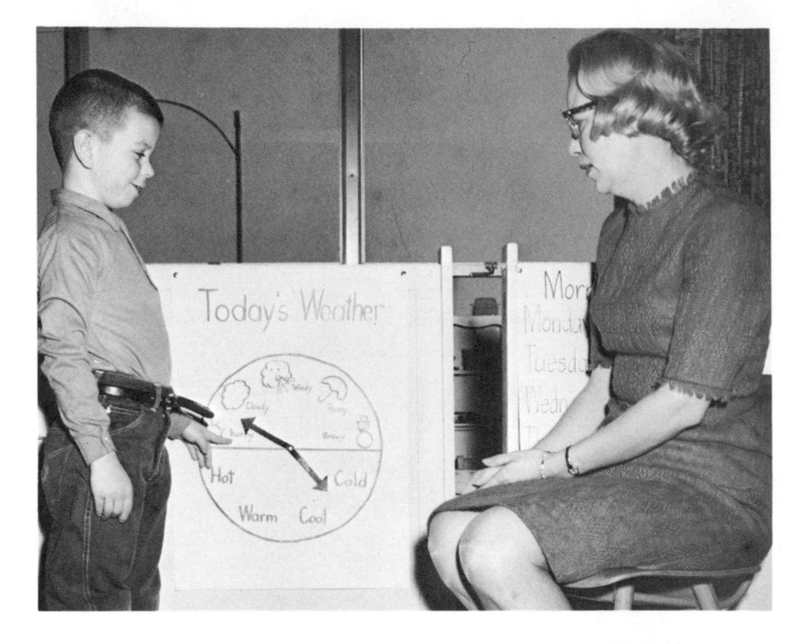

Machines
Melinda brought a paper-
cutting machine.
The needle is long, thin,
and sharp.
Turning the wheel makes
the needle cut.
Melinda cut some
paper.

9. Help children gain security in reading. Since the content of the chart is known to the children and the mode of expression is, for the most part, their own, they find security in reading charts because they have a reasonable possibility of succeeding—an important assurance to a young child beginning to learn a difficult skill. This value has been criticized by some educators and reading specialists. The Bonds[2] express the fear that known content offers no possibility for "discovery." For the beginning reader, however, the discovery involved in mastering the skills of reading is enough, and discovery of many new ideas can wait until some fluency has been established with known ideas.

10. Help motivate reading on a natural basis. The personal involvement of children in the chart and its content makes a more formal lesson quite self-motivated. The young child has more interest in "I" and the "now" than in other people and other times. Here, too, it has been argued that children identify with book characters, saying "book characters become real, too."[3] This is true. However, for the development of skills of reading it might be logical to read first about oneself; when fluency is developed, apply that skill to reading about others.

11. Help provide a foundation for all the language arts. Many of the skills identified with the other language arts are initiated and developed.

DEVELOPMENTAL READING

In a developmental reading program, experience charts are used (1) to introduce concepts and vocabulary, (2) to give needed practice and drill through repetition of difficult vocabulary, (3) to supplement the use of the chalkboard in word analysis exercises, and (4) to provide material for individual, independent check on comprehension and other skills.

---

[2] Guy L. Bond and Eva Bond, *Teaching the Child to Read* (New York: The Macmillan Co., 1944), p. 108.

[3] *Ibid.*, p. 105.

Sally said, I want something.
Something for little Tim.
Sally and Tim want something.
(New words are: want
something)[4]

Find:

1. five short vowels.
2. five long vowels.
3. five consonant blends.
4. five silent letters.

How I Attack New Words

eight—I think of freight.
sold—I put s before old.
forgot—I know both parts of this word, and the meaning is easy.
corn—I blend hard c with or and add n. It makes a word I know.
press—I know dress so I use pr for dr.

[4] William S. Gray, Marian Monroe, A. Sterl Artley, May Hill Arbuthnot, *We Come and Go* (Chicago: Scott Foresman, 1956), pp. 15-18.

sled dog
Husky
lead dog
musher
twenty-mile freight race
area
enthusiastic
beloved (bi luv id)[5]

What word says the same thing?[6]

Work	can
See	work
Can	see
Oh	funny
Funny	oh

Charts are useful for developing concepts and vocabulary of recorded experiences of the children or for developing the concepts and vocabulary of commercially prepared materials.

Since many present-day classrooms are equipped with very little chalkboard space, you often must choose from among several important curriculum areas the one to put on the available chalkboard space. Plans for the day might be put on the board so that items

[5] William S. Gray, Marian Monroe, A. Sterl Artley, May Hill Arbuthnot, *Guidebook to Accompany More Days and Deeds* (Chicago: Scott Foresman, 1956), p. 39.

[6] William S. Gray, Marian Monroe, A. Sterl Artley, May Hill Arbuthnot, *Guidebook to Accompany We Work and Play* (Chicago: Scott Foresman, 1956), p. 132.

can be easily and neatly erased when accomplished. When chalkboard space is used for the daily schedule, the teacher might want to make charts of the new vocabulary to be developed in reading or another lesson for the day. More often, however, new vocabulary is developed from the chalkboard, and the extending experiences in reading or other areas must be printed on a more permanent type of surface such as a chart and located near children who will work independently using the chart.

REINFORCEMENT ACTIVITIES

1. Surprise Charts[7]

To give practice through repetition of difficult vocabulary, you can create stories using the basic vocabulary of a story just completed or currently being read. The "surprise chart" enables you to have children repeat the vocabulary for reinforcement while keeping interest in the stories at a high level.

[7] This term should be credited to M. E. Broom, *et al.*, *Effective Reading Instruction* (New York: McGraw-Hill Book Co., Inc., 1951).

We Play

"I can play," said Joe.
"I can run," said Mary.
"I can run up and down," said Bill and Jill.

Teachers find that the several readings of a story which are necessary in order for children to learn the vocabulary and to give each child a turn to read cause children to lose interest in the story and in reading as well. Rewriting the story on a chart, with the same vocabulary but a slightly changed plot that adds an element of surprise, often is enough to hold the interest of the children and provide the needed practice. You may do this by substituting the names of the children from the class in the story or by incorporating incidents involving children in the class along with the story characters. You might instead incorporate new characters such as animals, fairies, cowboys, spacemen, or television favorites. In order to do this successfully, you must know or have available to you a list of the vocabulary used in stories read by the children up to this time.

Dick Wants Help

"Oh, oh, oh," said Dick.
"I can not do this.
Come and help me, Jane.
Please come and help me.
This is for Mother."

Billy Helps Dick

"Oh," said Dick, "I can not do this."
"I can help," said Billy.
"Please come and help me," said Dick.
Billy said, "I can help you do this
for Mother."

Memorization, a further problem that arises when repeated readings of material are necessary, can be checked through the use of "surprise stories." While memorization is a natural way for children to learn and the reliance upon memory of large units lasts normally for only a brief period, surprise charts are a useful means of preventing or checking this tendency.

2. Practice Activities

Many of the reinforcing activities suggested in teachers' manuals that accompany a basic developmental reading series can be put on charts and used by the group doing that work in class and later as independent work. Similarly, a teacher who is using original class-made chart materials for basic reading instruction can make adaptations of ideas suggested in teachers' guidebooks for extending and reinforcing activities. Examples of this kind of activity include the use of riddles to check comprehension.

What is it?

It is big.
It is not here.
It can go up, up, up.
What is it?

a ball a pin a rocket

Another chart reinforces the use of phonetic principles in word building and analysis.[8]

What words have the same vowel sound?[9]

sly	been
since	thought
caught	touch
grew	bite
hung	too

Other suggestions include questions to be answered,

What can you put in this bag?

A toy duck	A big white Bunny
Father's hat	A big boat
Seven candles	A little blue mouse
A yellow ball	Seven toy trains
Nan's hat	A green book
Something to eat	A birthday cake

---

[8] R. A. Swenson, "Phonic Charts," *Grade Teacher*, 68:34 (September, 1950).
[9] William S. Gray, Marian Monroe, A. Sterl Artley, May Hill Arbuthnot, *Guidebook to Accompany More Friends and Neighbors* (Chicago: Scott Foresman, 1956), p. 217.

Yes or No?

1. Is November a warm month?
2. Does Halloween come in November?
3. Does Thanksgiving come soon?
4. Does Veterans Day celebrate a fun day?
5. Do we come to school on Thanksgiving Day?

words to be classified,

Analogies

overshoe,	shoe;	________,	dress.
path,	road;	________,	clock.
eggs,	Easter;	________,	Christmas.
noon,	lunch;	________,	breakfast.

(apron, watch, presents, morning)[10]

or written instructions to be followed.

Read your story.
Divide it into scenes of action.
Describe the setting for each scene.
Write the dialogue for Scene I.

[10] *Ibid.*, p. 201.

Often this type of chart is general enough in nature to be kept and reused each year.

ENRICHMENT OF READING PROGRAM

At every level in the elementary school, experience charts can be used to extend and enrich the reading program. Often the ideas for the cooperatively developed reading materials are generated in a social studies or science unit in progress. This kind of work essentially provides for differences in reading ability among children in that a wider vocabulary is employed; words used are unique to the locale or a unit of work. At the same time, however, materials can be developed to enrich the reading program in which a regular developmental series is being used.

The Harry Smith

At the harbor, we saw a tug and a barge. Then we went aboard the Coast Guard cutter, Harry Smith. We saw the galley, the engines, and the guns.

A ten-year-old child who spent a summer in Paul Bunyan country wrote an account of a Paul Bunyan feat he heard related at the lodge; he could add a story to the reading unit on "Tall Tales."

The Big Darkness

One day Paul Bunyan and Babe, the Blue Ox, stepped from Maine to Minnesota. This happened at high noon. A vast shadow fell over all of eastern Canada. People thought the end of the world had come.

A group of children interested in old cars read materials on this topic and reported their findings in chart form for the class to read in connection with a unit centering on transportation.

Little material is available on current ideas such as our orbiting satellites. Children can write real or imaginary material on such topics.

Major Grissom and Commander Young are men who go into space. They are going to go to space now. 10-9-8-7-6-5-4-3-2-1-0 blast.

Some holidays are observed in stereotyped or limited ways. At any level, a chart record of significant aspects of holidays—as a result of reading research, interviewing, or describing individual family traditions—would make fine reading material which would yield worthwhile information and would be of high interest to children. Imaginative stories also, written by children, are more easily motivated at holiday times than at almost any other time of the school year.

Veterans Day

In the 1920's and 1930's Veterans Day was an important holiday. It was known as Armistice Day.

A dramatization of a reading story, rewritten if necessary, can be made using charts, much as "cue cards" are used on television.

A resourceful teacher with a group of imaginative children can develop and use many interesting reading materials.

SUMMARY

Charts can be used in a reading program to develop reading readiness concepts and skills, introduce, stimulate, and reinforce developmental reading programs, enrich the concepts and develop the imagination of children.

Chapter Five

Charts for Planning and Recording Units of Experience

If you enjoy planning with children you will find charts enjoyable and useful. Charts are valuable tools to assist in planning and organizing teaching around problems or large areas of study. These problems or areas of study may extend beyond one day's lesson and may involve the work and contribution of more than one child.

If a group of children can express verbally and write down for clarification and restatement the problem to be studied, the questions for which they want to get answers, their plans for procedure, a teacher has *greater assurance* that the purposes which should direct their learning activities are much clearer in their minds than if their conceptions had not been verified and tested. Teachers know how easily children can go off in all directions even though they are all supposed to be reading the same page or all attending to the question the teacher has just asked or written on the chalkboard. In fact, it is hard to see how a teacher can develop teaching units with her children without making extensive and continuous use of charts to crystallize plans, record data, consolidate experiences, and objectify criteria for observation and evaluation.

Charts to assist in the planning and developing of teaching units can be used as effectively at the intermediate and junior high level as at the primary level. In fact, anyone working with adult and community groups knows the value of the chalkboard as a focus for planning and for recording the work of the group as a basis for subsequent planning.

In chart writing as a part of a teaching unit, you will find it is helpful to use the chalkboard or easel for on-the-spot writing since statements and plans are tentative and subject to considerable change and modification as the plans mature and crystallize. The flexibility and convenience of the chalkboard with its easy-to-erase surface and potentialities for reorganization give it high standing for this use. As plans are made firm and commitments are made, however, charts which can be preserved, stored, and used conveniently many times have high priority. Here newsprint and tagboard charts reveal their value. Moreover, as the group works on its project and its several aspects you will want to preserve the records and notes of the group secretary or recorder; the notes, outlines, and substantive writing of each child should be kept also, on an individual basis. Thus chart writing in the development of a teaching unit should involve the chalkboard, easel writing on tagboard and newsprint, and individual writing on regular size paper and in notebooks. The function of each and the relationship that ought to exist among the different writing media should be kept clear and exploited fully. It is wise for a skillful teacher to avail herself of the contribution all three make to the group and individual writing of her children.

In order to help you see how the chart writing becomes an important and essential part of planning with children, we will follow one teacher and her group of third grade children through the development of a class unit on "Birds in Our Community." We are sure you will recognize how you can begin, even in a small way, to incorporate the use of this tool in your own teaching.

BIRDS IN OUR COMMUNITY [1]

The school room is located on the protected side of the school near a wooded area. "Living Things" is the large area of study for the science program. Children in this group are familiar with birds —they see them when going to and from school, and on weekends in parks.

The Teacher Writes Plans. The unit could start in many ways; this teacher, although working within the assigned area of "Living Things," had some flexibility in choice—pets, birds, worms, etc. Birds were selected by the teacher as having high educational potential; she is now confronted with the decision of how to start. A nest, a feather, picture, questions of children, and field trip were considered possibilities. She listed her goals for this unit:

1. Observation of the objects that exist and phenomena that take place in his environment and ability to report accurately what he observes.
2. Skill in evaluating the relative importance and the relevancy or irrelevancy of the data to a situation.
3. Evaluation of the information to determine if there is enough to warrant making a tentative answer.
4. Ability to decide on the most efficient way to obtain the needed information.
5. Development of attitudes of:
   a. kindness and respect for all living things.
   b. awareness of the world about him.
   c. respect for the ideas of others.
   d. desire to conserve birds for beauty as well as use.

You may write down other things to help you in your planning. Most importantly, remember that plans explicitly thought through by the teacher, and some aspects of them written down, will help greatly to give direction to teaching just as plans prepared by the teacher and her children will help to develop and make them explicit as tools for further group thinking and work.

Here We Go!

First Day. (A cold day in February.) A child coming back to school from lunch at home says, "I saw a bird on the way to

---

[1] Courtesy of Mrs. Meryl Parchmann.

school. What does he eat in such cold weather with the ground frozen?" Other children gather around and wonder about it, too.

Teacher: "How do you think we could find out?"
Ann: "We could ask someone or look it up in a book."
Bill: "I have seen bird feeders in some yards. Why don't we find out about them?"
Bob: "Maybe we could place a shelf on the window?"

The discussion indicated that they ought to find out more about bird feeders before going ahead with their plans.

They thought of asking brothers, fathers, an industrial arts teacher and consulting books in the library. They were eager to get busy. This summarizing led to the first charts: (a) a question chart and (b) a chart of assignment of responsibilities.

Things to Find Out About Bird Feeders

1. What kind?
2. Could we build one?

Things to Do

1. Ask parents—Everyone
2. Ask older brother—John, Bill
3. Ask custodian—Bob, Ralph
4. Ask industrial arts teacher—Craig, Ronny
5. Look up in books—Alice, Arlene, Lucille

Sometimes it comes out like this—sometimes not. The point is that the interaction among children and between children and their teacher in the form of discussion, questions, conversations, and work activities provides an excellent base for unit planning and chart writing.

Since this is a relatively short time assignment of responsibility, the chalkboard is an excellent medium.

The teacher here served as recorder. At upper levels, one of the children can serve as writer. Later in the project children in this group can assist in the writing.

Second Day. The children reported and their findings were placed on the chalkboard.

Our Findings

1. Industrial arts teacher—could help build one but it would take time.
2. Custodian—offered to put up simple shelf.
3. Parents—offered to build feeders.

Children's building plans were a little complicated but a simple shelf was decided upon.

The discussion then turned to food and they were interested in finding out what the birds liked best. Another list of responsibilities was developed on "Food to Bring."

Food to Bring

1. Stale bread—Jane
2. Stale cake—Alice
3. Sunflower seeds—Bill
4. Apple—Bob
5. Raisins—Sally
6. Chopped nuts—Jo
7. Cracked corn—Amy
8. Water container—John

Discussion went on about handling of the food.

Teacher: "Who is going to put the feed out?"
Bob: "Why not take turns? Maybe two people a day and we could go by our seat rows."
Teacher: "If you will bring the food in plastic containers or something that will not tear or break, we will start our feeder in the morning."

It should be clear here that responsibilities that carry over more than one day or information that is going to be used for an extended period of time should be a cue for more permanent charts than the chalkboard list.

Third Day. The feeder is in place. Children bring their food and place it on the counter. They were all at school a little earlier than usual and spent this time deciding that they would try a little of each kind of food. Water was put out and concern was evidenced over the possibility that it might freeze and what this would do. The discussion then moved to—

Jo: "What shall we do when we see a bird?"
Bill: "We can write it down so we can remember."
Teacher: "That is a good suggestion. What do you think we should write?"
Amy: "The kind of bird. If we don't know the kind we can write the description and then look it up in a book."
Bob: "Let's try to see what the bird eats."
Sue: "How about checking the time to see if they come more often at certain times of the day?"
Teacher: "We have a number of things to watch for. Let's write them down so we all can use them in our watching of birds."

Can you see the need developing here for a common list of things these children wish to observe about birds and their habits? This *common agreement* on characteristics to observe is an important part of the scientific method.

An important responsibility of the teacher is to see that these characteristics are identified, are made available for use by all children, are used to direct observation, make records, and draw conclusions. Chart writing is helpful in this.

Things to Watch

1. Date.
2. The kind of bird.
3. Description of bird if in doubt—coloring, shape, bill.
4. What the bird eats.
5. Does it like water.
6. What foods are left on the shelf.
7. What time of day.

Teacher: "Do you know what we call writing down things of importance?"
John: "Keeping a record. Let's make a bird folder and call it our bird unit or bird record."
Teacher: "We will keep one chart for reference but each of you can copy the questions for your folder."
Bill: "Why don't the two boys that take care of the feeder keep the record for that day and we can copy it in science class. Or we all can keep the record and then check."
Teacher: "What do you think we are going to find out by keeping this record?"
Ronny: "The kinds of birds that stay during the winter."
Teacher: "Why don't we watch and see. We will check in a week."

Notice how children, themselves, start to see the need for records, how different ways can be explored for keeping them, and how checking of such records can be done.

Fourth Day. The weather is mild and only sparrows have come to the feeder. There is some discussion as to why other birds do not come.

Bill: "It hasn't been long. We are in too much of a rush."

Fifth Day. Work on folders and do library reading on birds.

It should be clear here that a group chart supports and encourages the individual study and writing of children in class.

Each kind of writing should be seen in its relationship to other forms and uses for writing. No one kind of writing stands alone as a tool for meeting all writing purposes.

The Following Week

There was a big snowstorm over the weekend. On Monday children came armed with food and lots of enthusiasm. One brought a bird feeder to put on a tree, another child brought some suet and a wire holder. They decided to stock each feeder with the same food.

Someone mentioned cats. After discussion, the children decided to take the feeder down if a cat should appear.

During the discussion, a cardinal flew to the window and the children rushed to the window. The bird flew away. The children were greatly concerned.

Teacher: "Do you know why the bird flew away?"
Children: "We frightencd it away."
Teacher: "What shall we do about this?"

Discussion brought out the importance of not making sudden movements, keeping quiet, and not going too close to the window if birds were not to be scared away.

No one bothered to make this chart. Apparently these points were clear and highly significant to every child. *No need to belabor this learning.*

Two Weeks Later

Teacher: "Have we learned anything about birds and what they eat here in the winter?"
Bill: "We have watched for several days. It took a long time for birds to come but they finally found our feeders."
Alice: "Let's check our records."
Teacher: "I'll write down on the board the things we found. Let's take turns reading our records for our list."

Our Findings

1. Kinds of birds: Cardinal, Sparrow, Junco, Chickadee, Downy Woodpecker
2. Description: We looked these up each day so we would know the bird if it came again.
3. What the birds ate: Couldn't tell which bird ate what—but all the food was gone.
4. Did birds like water: Yes
5. What foods were left on the shelf: None
6. What time of day did birds come: Early morning and later in the afternoon
7. Suet feeder: Chickadees

Teacher: "What are some of the things we have found out? Will each one write your contribution on the board so we can see how our learnings add up."

Bob: "It took a long time for the birds to come."

Bill: "There were more sparrows than any other bird with cardinals, juncos, chickadees, and downy woodpeckers in that order."

Ken: "We could not tell the food each separate bird liked the best except the suet feeders—the chickadee and the downy woodpecker."

Ivy: "They ate all the food and they all drank water."

Sue: "There were more birds in the afternoon and earlier in the morning, but they came all through the day."

Can you see how these generalizations may be checked with exceptions and conditions noted? We would suggest that children not write their names next to their generalizations when writing for a group. Generalizations can be changed and improved more easily without this personal referent. The whole class can look at these statements, check with records and readings, and change and modify them until they are satisfied with their rightness.

Teacher: "Have we learned anything else that we ought to write down and remember?"
Bob: "We need patience and cannot jump to conclusions."
Alice: "From the number of birds counted there were more at the tree feeder. They were probably afraid of the building and felt safer in trees."
Ronny: "The cardinal and junco came more often to the window. So, they are probably the more friendly or less timid of all the birds."

The children are starting to consider causes behind the conclusions. Notice how they express "could it be" hypotheses about why the birds behaved as they did.

Teacher: "Do you believe we have watched long enough?"
Bob: "The birds are used to coming and might miss our food. Let's keep it up until warm weather."

The children agreed that this was a good idea but had a number of questions.

Teacher: "Let's write down some of your questions so we can use them in any further study of birds."

Further Questions

1. Do birds have teeth? They can crack seeds with their bills.
2. Are males and females colored differently? Two cardinals were colored differently.
3. Do different kinds of birds build different kinds of nests and put them in different places? We observed different kinds of nests.
4. Some birds go away during the winter. Where do they go? When do they come back?
5. We read about hummingbirds, robins, orioles. Can we study them?

These questions growing honestly out of their study are invaluable curriculum materials for the teacher and children. You do not have to answer these questions on the spot but you do need to keep a record of them, refer to them when work is related to them, and use the list to pinpoint and plan future learning activities in this area.

All things have to have certain periods placed on them. Many teachers use a bulletin board as a place where the children can bring together pictures of birds, the things they have learned, and titles and headings are made to organize the display.

Teacher: "We have a long list of questions. Let's keep them on our planning chart as things to keep in mind. Some of them will be answered as we do other things. Some we will want to come back to when spring comes and the rest of the birds return."

Children do not object to this kind of planning. After all, they have the tangible evidence before their eyes. As a teacher, however, you had better come back and account for these questions.

SUMMARY

You have seen how the development of a unit with children has given rise to needs for records of agreements on purposes to be achieved, questions to be answered, assignments of responsibilities, records of observations, summaries of data, listing of tentative findings and conclusions, and the building of an agenda of unsolved questions for future work and study. We have seen, too, how group charts provide the basis for individual notes, records, and summaries and, conversely, how the individual notes and writings provide the basis for the group summary chart in which the work and contributions of the unit are consolidated.

At times the writing of the group chart was obviously the responsibility of the teacher. At others individual children would need to do the writing. Some charts were clearly necessary only for the moment, others needed to be used for a number of purposes over an extended period of time—thus the chalkboard, newsprint, and tagboard materials need to be used flexibly and appropriately. There were times, too, when the learning was so clear and definite that trying to write a chart or make a list on the chalkboard was redundant—there was no need to belabor the obvious with either children or adults.

Chapter Six

Problems of Readability

Readability of materials, or the ease with which material can be read, can be controlled through the interest and difficulty factors of material and suitable format. The first step toward developing readable materials is knowledge of the audience for whom you are writing. As a classroom teacher, you are in an advantageous position to develop truly readable materials. A listing and description of important factors follows, with examples.

INTERESTS OF CHILDREN

Enough is known about interests of children in general so that your charts can be stimulating to children as well as designed to provide opportunities for their development of reading and other skills.

The following generalizations are known about children's interests.

Interests of children are acquired.

Children can expand their interests.

Interests vary with the maturity of the child.

Interests vary with the nature of his home and community.

Children of any age like materials centering around: people, personal relationships; self; hobbies; animals; adventure, exploration; experimentation; surprise; humor; and information, "how to do it."

Increasingly as he grows older the sex of a child makes a difference in his interests.

Generally not liked by children of any age is material with a heavy moral tone.

Young girls and boys have similar interests. At about age nine or sometimes earlier, interests of boys and girls tend to become differentiated. For example, girls may transfer their interest in dolls and fairies to career and home. Boys are likely to concentrate on adventure and sports. Since it is difficult for a boy to adopt a girl's interest, but not so difficult for a girl to become involved in a boy's interest, when you must make a choice, more children will be interested if the boys' interest is selected.

VOCABULARY DIFFICULTY

You can do a lot about varying the vocabulary load of the experience charts you help write.

Vocabulary difficulty is basically of two kinds: word recognition and idea comprehension.

Word Recognition

Word recognition becomes a problem when many different, hard, or uncommon words appear in a given sample of reading material. You can control this by limiting the number of different words used, and by repeating words. Use of a few uncommon words, however, adds character to a selection. And it must be kept in mind that one of the functions of charts is to expand vocabulary rather than restrict it. The following example,[1] an excerpt from a second-grade class project in science, illustrates how some difficult words and ideas can be mastered by elementary grade children.

The Sun

While the earth is turning it's turning around the sun. If the earth were closer to the sun it would blow up to bits for the sun is a ball of whirling gases. If we could live on the sun we would be in the midst of thousands of explosions hotter than the hottest stove in the world. You'd weigh more than all the children in your class put together! This is because the sun's gravity is stronger than the earth's gravity. Sometimes the moon covers up the sun and everything grows dark. This is called an "eclipse" which means hiding something. If an airplane got too close to the sun its metal body would boil.

The sun helps the earth by heating it and making clouds.

Hard words are often defined as polysyllabic words. Professional writers use reading formulas which provide for difficulty factors inherent in polysyllabic words and different words through systems of numerical weighting. You, too, can take these factors into account when preparing charts.

Word Lists. It is important that teachers recognize what words are basic to reading materials and the oral language of children.

[1] From *The Able Learner,* Superintendent's Annual Report, Cincinnati Public Schools, 1957-1958, p. 24.

One source that can be of help to teachers is the word lists prepared by researchers.

Word lists are generally made up of words taken from children's books—trade and text; adult literature—classics, vocational-technical, newspapers, letters; children's conversation or writing, or words children can define or otherwise identify. If you plan to use a word list you should know the source of the words in that list and use words from the list in material or activities of that kind.

Length and Use. A word list of ten, twenty, or thirty thousand words is cumbersome and time consuming for you to use. Such a list has the further disadvantage of tempting the teacher to refer to it and uncritically to substitute for some hard word an easy one that may change real or intended meanings and detract from the character of the selection. Notice how this sentence loses color and precision in the second version.

The pony loped around the corral.
The little horse ran in the ring.

It is suggested that you use a simple word list, such as that in the basic reading series used by your school. For completeness and interest, you can add the necessary words from the ideas and experiences of the children.

Speaking Vocabulary. The words your children use in conversations, recitations, and discussions should be studied carefully and used and extended in chart writing. In working with bilingual learners, either children or adults, the Eaton Semantics Frequency List[2] is a convenient reference for finding words in French, German, or Spanish that are similar in meaning to words in English.

---

[2] Helen Eaton, *Semantic Frequency List for English, French, German, and Spanish* (Chicago: University of Chicago Press, 1940).

Comprehension of Ideas

Experience charts written with children can aid you in teaching children to understand ideas expressed in written form. If you pay close attention to the way in which your children express ideas, you will recognize that materials which are easier to comprehend are characterized by the use of (1) more concrete ideas, (2) experiences familiar to your children, and (3) direct writing.

Words having concrete meaning give a clearer impression and hold the attention of children longer than more general and abstract words.

Trade

As in the Middle Ages, people today trade ideas, goods, and good will.

We send the Peace Corps to help other people learn how to read and write and help them gain knowledge of how to raise crops. For this we get nothing material in return.

We buy tin from South America and uranium from Africa. In return, they get farm machinery, materials to build schools, and dollars to pay teachers. In this trade we both benefit.

War and peace may be affected by trade. A people is not likely to pick a fight with us if they want our goods. We, too, trade all over the world so we are not likely to pick a fight as we need these countries' goods.

The problem of multiple meanings of words occurs as a complicating factor, making apparently simple nouns and verbs much less simple upon closer scrutiny. The classic example of this is the many meanings of the word "run."

Run for President.
Run to the store.
Run in my stocking.
Run into the door.
etc.

Familiar experiences are those close to children in time and space. This familiarity can be achieved through either real or vicarious experience. The younger the child, the more limited his interest and experience in other places, other times, and people in a different age group, and the more his concerns are with here, now, I, me, my, and mine.

The direct approach can be achieved in several ways. Material addressed to the reader, use of personal pronouns and pronouns denoting gender, use of dialogue, familiar word order, dramatic expression, vigorous style, positive phrasing, and use of simple time sequence provide high readability.

THIS
You will notice that on a hot day you perspire. If you suddenly feel very warm and are not perspiring, say "Stop!" to yourself. Get help.

NOT THIS
Heat stroke is the result of overheating the body. The heat regulating mechanisms of the body break down, temperature rises very rapidly.

On the other hand, difficult materials are those that employ abstract ideas, grammatical form not used by children, and a high concentration of ideas with little description or explanation. Unusual word order also gives difficulty. In general, the more prepositions and prepositional phrases you have, the more difficult the material will be for children to comprehend.

SENTENCE STRUCTURE

The length and complexity of the sentence is another factor influencing readability. You can appraise the complexity of sentence structure by observing the average sentence length.

Average Sentence Length

Grade 1:	8 words
2:	10 words
3:	12 words
4:	13 words
5:	14 words
6:	15 words

Longer sentences tend to be more complex sentences and are read more slowly and with more difficulty since greater duration of attention is demanded and because more complex sentences generally are used to express more complex ideas. Short sentences permit rapid reading, though too many short sentences soon become monotonous. A recommended procedure is the use of a balance of short and long sentences, using short sentences for force and emphasis, and longer ones for summary of details.

FORM

Most charts are in narrative form, either factual in nature or imaginative. Next in use are charts employing lists of words or questions, particularly vocabulary lists and information-seeking questions in connection with unit work.

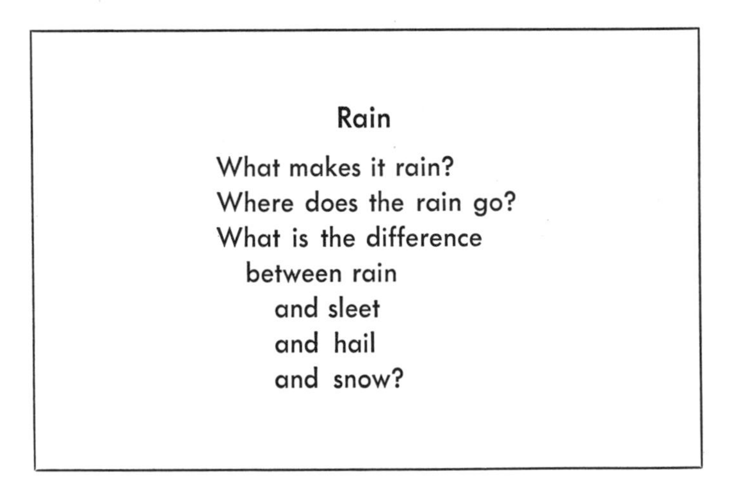

Occasionally the form of a poem or song chart, using other types of symbols, may be introduced.

LINE ARRANGEMENT

Problems in writing the sentences down include the problem of spacing and alignment: (a) placement and alignment of sentences on the chart; (b) spacing of letters in the word, words in sentences, sentences in relation to each other, and (c) paragraphs.

For the beginning reader, each sentence serves as a paragraph and each sentence should be an unbroken visual unit. As the reader matures, he is able to hold on to an idea, make the return sweep, and add to the idea. When longer sentences are used which need to be broken at the end of a line, they should be broken between phrases. Not until a child reaches the intermediate grade reading level should a word be divided.

The child's capacity in relation to the idea to be presented also places limits to line length. When a long line causes the reader to become lost on the return sweep, it is desirable to shorten the line by division. A two-column arrangement of print divided by a vertical line, or "rule," is just as effective an arrangement as a greater space between the columns.

The size of the paper on which the chart is recorded should not, but often does, limit you in length of the line to be recorded. When writing on the chalkboard this is no problem, and a very long line is possible. The size of the chart depends on the use: a booklet for individual use—9″ x 18″; for board or easel use—18″ x 36″. As a general rule, the greater the distance between the reader and the material to be read, the longer the line that is possible.

The sentence should be balanced to the chart size and shape. Naturally the lines on this sample chart are not easy to read.

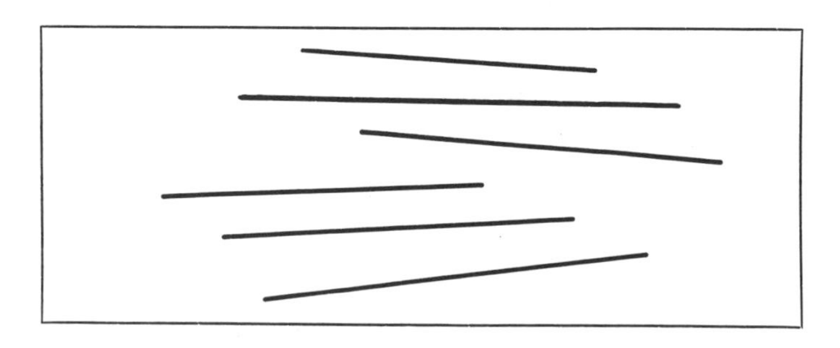

Letters in words and words in sentences should be grouped as a unit.

Keep letters closely spaced.

NOT	BUT
p on y	pony

Keep spacing between words even.

NOT

One   wheel was   off .

BUT

One wheel was off .

Keep lines evenly spaced. You may have to draw guidelines to help you.

NOT

It is big and round.
It would take 200 eggs.

We have an incubator.

BUT

It is big and round.
It would take 200 eggs.
We have an incubator.

Double space between paragraphs.

NOT

Pigs live in a pig pen.
They eat corn.
A mother chicken is a hen.
She lays eggs.

BUT

Pigs live in a pig pen.
They eat corn.

A mother chicken is a hen.
She lays eggs.

You will note the following styles.

A SERIES OF SENTENCES OF SIMILAR LENGTH

This is a fox's house.
It is on top of the hill.
Four foxes live here.

THE INCOMPLETE SENTENCE

A chicken can
walk.
fly.
run.
peck.
peep.

THE RUN-OVER SENTENCE

The crooked cat and the crooked mouse live in this
house, too.

You will need to watch the phrasing so that the thought units are not broken.

Today, Jimmy brought some
frog eggs.

You will want to pay attention to good phrasing here, too.

THE PARAGRAPH FORM

Cows and Milk

We went to the farm. We saw a large herd of cows.

The farmer drove them into a barn. The man washed their udders. He attached the milking machines.

The milk ran through glass pipes to large tanks. These tanks were cooled by cold water.

PICTURES

Conventionally, illustrations representing the total chart are placed near the top center of the chart, with an ample allowance for margins. Smaller illustrations may be placed at the bottom of the page or along the right hand margin of the chart.

TITLE

The title should be kept short, centered above the text of the chart, and printed somewhat larger than the text of the chart. The first letter of important words should be capitalized. The spaces above and below the title should be slightly greater than the spaces between lines of the text.

SIZE AND NATURE OF WRITING

The printing, manuscript lettering, or writing should be legible and aesthetically pleasing. The proper size and formation of letters help. Clear distinctions must be made between capital and small letters. Lower-case letters, with capitals used where they are conventionally used, should be the style. Any use of mixed type demands reader adjustments that slow his reading speed.

A simple form of lettering or writing is to be preferred to an ornate type. A sample of lower-case and capital letters will be found in the Appendix, page 116.

A broad, heavy, uniform stroke enhances legibility. The stroke is well proportioned if its width is about 18% (1/6) the height of the total letter. A heavy stroke ensures a sharper image.

Sharp contrasts with the paper background help make a chart more readable.

Letters should be large enough to be read from the greatest distance at which the chart will be viewed. Lettering at least 1½ to 2 inches high is desirable.

Space between words should be in proportion to the size of print, with a minimum space of one inch. Spacing between lines should be ample with 3/8-inch minimum whether the print is small or large.

Margins serve to keep the reader's attention on the page. Varying in width from one to three inches, margins occupy approximately one-half of the surface on the page.

LENGTH

A chart should be long enough to say what needs to be said. Generally, young children tend to develop charts four or five sentences long. Older children may develop charts of several pages.

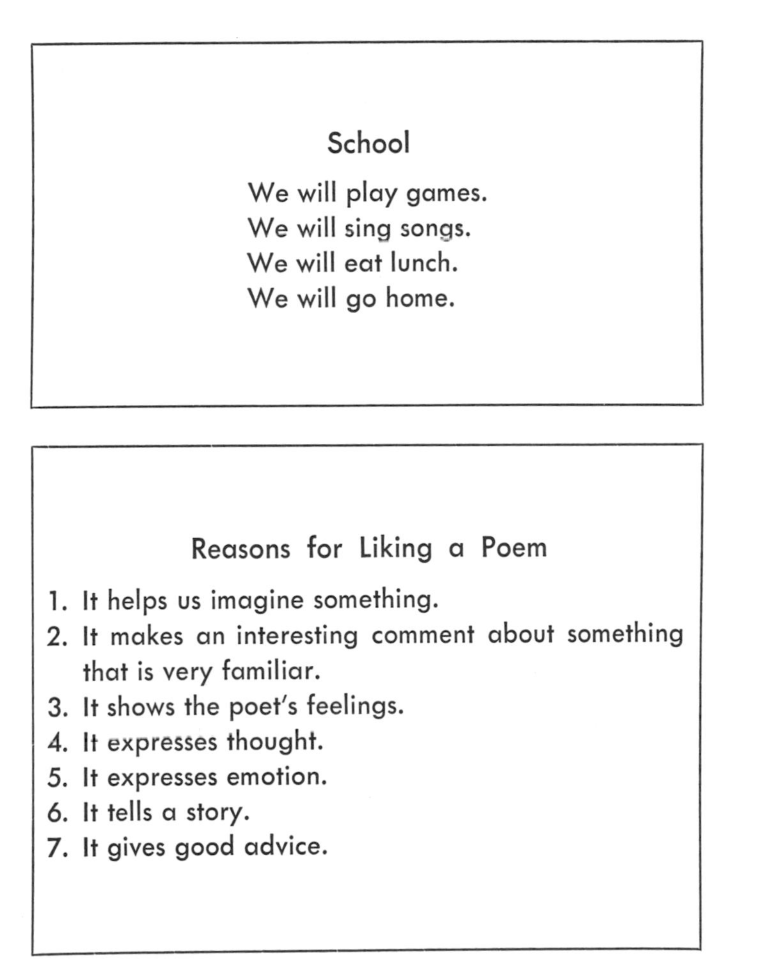

School

We will play games.
We will sing songs.
We will eat lunch.
We will go home.

Reasons for Liking a Poem

1. It helps us imagine something.
2. It makes an interesting comment about something that is very familiar.
3. It shows the poet's feelings.
4. It expresses thought.
5. It expresses emotion.
6. It tells a story.
7. It gives good advice.

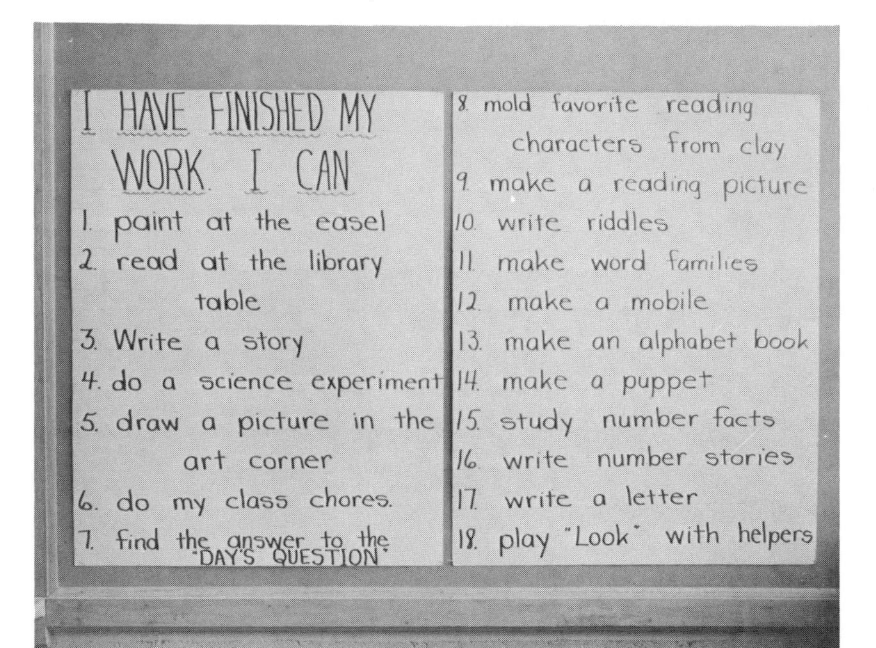
I HAVE FINISHED MY WORK I CAN
1. paint at the easel
2. read at the library table
3. Write a story
4. do a science experiment
5. draw a picture in the art corner
6. do my class chores.
7. find the answer to the "DAY'S QUESTION"
8. mold favorite reading characters from clay
9. make a reading picture
10. write riddles
11. make word families
12. make a mobile
13. make an alphabet book
14. make a puppet
15. study number facts
16. write number stories
17. write a letter
18. play "Look" with helpers

THE NUTCRACKERS
The Nutcracker Triplets
One day there was a knock on the Williams' door. Cary and Ivy rushed to open it. When the children saw the mailman with a large box, they were excited, curious and impatient. The three children help their mother open the package that Aunt Dee had sent from Germany.
For Cary there was a nutcracker that looked like Heidi's grandfather.
Ivy's nutcracker resembled Hansel and Gretel's mother_only she has a big smile.
Tracy, Cary's little brother, was very excited when he saw his nutcracker that looked like the soldier in The Nutcrack Suite.
The nutcracker triplets were all hand carved in Germany.
Sonny
Sonny
Sonny

SUMMARY

Readability factors include those factors involving (1) the materials used in chart making and their suitability, and (2) the psychological factors of level of difficulty and appeal to the learner. We hope you can apply some of the ideas discussed to your own chart writing.

Chapter Seven

Materials and Equipment for Chart Writing

Materials and equipment for chart making include provisions for writing, displaying, and possibly storing charts. Schools generally provide materials and equipment that you can use with complete

satisfaction in making and using charts. In other instances you can adapt materials for chart use. Some places where special chart materials may be obtained are suggested in this chapter.

THE SURFACE

You have seen that very often you will use the chalkboard for recording during the planning of the chart.

Chalkboard Checklist:

Chalkboard
Chalk
Eraser
Liner

Sources:

Adjustable Staff Liner MB[1]

You may use the chalkboard because it is accessible to the view of children at all times and revisions of the chart can conveniently be made on this easy-to-clean surface.

Some school classrooms, however, have limited chalkboard space and it is possible that your next activity will require the use of the chalkboard, so you or a child will need to record the chart-in-progress on a more permanent surface. You may prefer to record the first draft of a chart on easel size newsprint, either unruled or with a one-inch ruling. When newsprint is not available, wrapping paper may be substituted if your writing tool makes a clear image on the paper.

Paper Checklist:

Easel Paper (ruled or unruled; rolls or sheets; colored or natural)
- Newsprint
- Bond
- Art
- Tagboard
- Poster board

Sources:

Newsprint: 28½″, 275 lineal feet (roll) FL
Art Paper: 24″, 180 lineal feet (roll) FL
Bond Tablet: 24″ x 16″ (1″ rule, 24″ way), 25 sheets FL
  30 sheets (punched) FL

---

[1] Names and addresses of suppliers represented here by abbreviations will be found at the end of this chapter.

Primary Chart Paper (pad):
- 18″ x 24″ (ruled 24″ way) (100 sheets) FL
- 24″ x 36″ (ruled 36″ way) (100 sheets) FL
- 24″ x 36″ (ruled 24″ way) (100 sheets) FL

Ruled Music Chart Roll (Newsprint):
- 28″ wide x 250″ long (4 staffs long way, ¾″ space) BC
- 28″ wide x 250″ long (1½″ ruling, plain other side) FD

Newsprint 224″ x 36″ (500 sheets) MET
Kraft Paper 24″ x 36″ (100 sheets) MET
Manilla Oak Tag 24″ x 36″ (25, 100, 500 sheets; heavy or light quality) MET
White Coated Board 22″ x 28″ (100 sheets; heavy or light quality) MET

For the completed chart you may use tagboard, poster board, or newsprint. Charts that you plan to use over a considerable time or charts that will be handled by children can be recorded on tagboard because of its durability. For the occasional chart that is to be relatively permanent in a classroom, poster board is used. For most uses, however, natural or tinted newsprint is entirely satisfactory. The importance of the paper color depends largely upon its relation to the brightness contrast provided by the writing instrument. Newsprint charts if hung on frames, chalkboards, or easels need to have either their hanging edge reinforced with a strip of tagboard attached with rubber cement or holes reinforced with linen eyelets. Otherwise, clips, rings, and hangers will soon tear the paper if the charts are turned over frequently.

THE INSTRUMENT

Of course chalk and the chalkboard eraser are used when a chart is being recorded on the chalkboard. When the writing surface is paper, you have more choice.

Writing Instrument Checklist:

- Crayon
- Pen
  - Felt-tip
  - Steel nib
  - Lettering set

Sources:

Esterbrook Drawlet Pens MET
Sanford's Dry Line Pen MET
Flo-Master Felt Tip Pens
(4 nibs and ink) BC, FL
Marsh 77 Felt Point Pen
(2 extra points, ink) BC, FL
Speedball Lettering Sets
(9 pens, ink, holder, book
of instructions) BC, FL, MET

Lettering Sets

Manuscript Type Chart Printer
(letters, punctuation,
ruler, and guide bar;
4 sizes) BC

Ordinary wax crayon is a convenient instrument to handle, making it equally useful for first or final draft. Particularly for the final draft of a chart, many people feel that no instrument produces as clear an image as the broad-point pen used with India ink. This medium, however, is often difficult to manage, and errors are more difficult to correct.

A lettering set and ink pad were universally used in chart making before manuscript writing came into popular use. Many teachers still feel that the accurately made letters and their close correspondence to "book print" make the use of lettering sets a wise choice.

The recent readily available felt-tip pens, often with self-contained ink supply in a choice of colors, combines the best features of each of the above.

MOUNTING

Special equipment is least likely to be available to you and is least necessary for mounting the chart. Such equipment can be secured from school supply houses, but teachers frequently use or adapt facilities already available in the classroom.

Mounting Checklist:

Map Rail
Thumb Tacks

Easel
Big Book
Bulletin Board
Masking Tape

Sources:

Map Display Rail (with sliding hangers) DG, MET

Easel (single or double, 3 heights) MB, FL, MET

Hanging Chart Rack BC, FL

Pegboard Screen (34″ x 50″) FL

Ideal Chart Stand (54″ high for chart 42″ long, 28″ wide for charts 26″ wide) BC, MET

Music Chart Rack (25 sheets of 48″ x 30″ tagboard, 4 staffs each side; container serves as easel and storage) BC

Teaching Chart and Rack Set (25 sheets tagboard 24″ x 30″, ruled one side, half of sheet ruled reverse side; cardboard stand, booklet of suggestions) BC FL

Charts and Tripod Set (12 sheets 24″ x 36″ manilla, metal chart-head, steel stand—adjustable, revolving tripod) BC

TV Scroll Viewer (24″ x 14″ screen in cardboard case with dial knobs; 12″ x 20′ manilla tag scroll with 1″ ruling in grey) BC

Exhibit Hooks BC

The cork and metal map rail with which many intermediate grade classrooms are equipped may be used for mounting charts, either by means of thumbtacking the chart or using rings or cord to hang the charts from the map hooks. The "machines" chart on page 64 also demonstrates this.

The painting easel found in most primary grade classrooms

can be an excellent portable chart holder. See also the second photograph on page 14 and the photograph on page 36.

The "big book" of pre-primer stories supplied by many of the publishers of developmental reading series can have additional chart pages inserted.

A bulletin board, too, can be used to mount a chart, either temporarily during the recording, or for later use. Masking tape may be used to attach a chart to the chalkboard.

Whatever mounting may be selected, the essential conditions are good lighting, accessibility to children, and steady mounting so the chart does not move when being used by children.

STORAGE

A chart can, having served its purpose, be discarded. In only occasional, very exceptional cases should a chart be preserved and used another year. Charts to be saved should be of general interest: a report of a significant incident that is not likely to occur again or otherwise be available, rewritten materials from the regular curriculum, or children's creativc efforts of high literary quality.

It can be filed or placed in a looseleaf binder with like materials, to be reused when needed. It can be reproduced on paper of a more convenient size for individuals to handle and taken home by children immediately or kept and bound in a collection of like materials to be taken home at the end of a given period.

For storage of charts that may have further usefulness, you will need a surface large enough for the chart to lie, hang, or stand flat, or you may roll the chart into a tube. Probably the best storage arrangement is a half a dozen or more shelves large enough to permit charts to lie flat, with no overlap. Many school supply rooms have shelves of this kind. The various shelves could be labeled and reserved for chart paper and completed charts not in use. Other possible arrangements include an envelope of heavy cardboard, a "big book" for chart storage as well as a chart holder, plastic bags such as those which protect clothing being delivered from the dry cleaners, or an especially built storage "box." [2]

Storage Checklist:

Tube
Envelope
Big Book
Shelves
Box

Sources:

Shelves: Educators Cabinets (fixed or movable) EM

AUXILIARY MATERIALS

When preparing to make a chart, in addition to the above materials and conditions, you would do well to have at hand a yardstick, a foot rule, a pencil for drawing guidelines, and an eraser. A music staff liner with chalk placed in the slots for the clef lines is an aid to the teacher for drawing straight and well spaced lines on the chalkboard.

Auxiliary Materials Checklist:

Yardstick
Foot Rule
Pencil
Eraser
Staff Liner or Chart Liner
Pocket Chart
Blank Word, Phrase Cards
Duplicator Carbons, Paper
Typewriter (with proper type)

Sources:

Card holder (34″ x 30½″ with pockets for words, phrases, or sentences) FL

[2] B. J. Hahn, "Chart Storage and Display," *Industrial Arts and Vocational Education,* November, 1956, p. 295.

If the chart is to be used for reading instruction, a card holder with pockets and blank word cards and phrase cards should be available. If you expect individual children to use the chart at their desks or at home, duplicating supplies and a typewriter with appropriate type size will be needed.

SUMMARY

Most classrooms have adequate materials and other provisions for chart making and use, or adaptations of present materials and facilities can be made. Specially designed equipment can be secured or made, however. You can obtain these specially designed materials from the sources suggested on the foregoing pages and below.

Sources of Materials for Constructing Charts

BC: Beckley-Cardy
1900 Narragansett
Chicago 39, Illinois

DG: Denoyer-Geppert Co.
5235 Ravenswood Ave.
Chicago 40, Illinois

EM: Educators Manufacturing Co.
P.O. Box 1261
Tacoma, Washington

FL: Fond du Lac School Supply Co.
School Buyer's Guide
Fond du Lac, Wisconsin

MB: Milton Bradley Co.
Springfield, Massachusetts
Distributor:
A. C. McClurg & Co., Inc.
333 East Ontario St.
Chicago 11, Illinois

MET: Metropolitan
School Buyer's Guide
Cedar Rapids, Iowa

A Checklist for Experience Chart Writing

You will want to include children in the selection and development of ideas for your charts.

You need to know well the language arts skills, children, and the curriculum in order to perform skillfully your roles in making and using charts.

Chart making and use is an exploratory process which interrelates language arts processes and the ideas from content fields.

The procedures of chart making include an experience, discussion, recording, and use.

Experiences suitable for charts may be individual or held in common by a group.

Children's interests are both known, therefore predictable, and capable of development.

Discussion clarifies ideas and builds vocabulary.

Recording the chart involves consideration of arrangement, writing, and illustrations.

Vocabulary control is possible.

Chart usefulness may be of limited or extended duration.

Charts may be used for keeping a record of a unit, for reading development or supplement, and for other language arts.

You have available to you in the usual school supplies all that you need for making, using, and storing charts.

Experience charts are called by many names; these names are less important than the varied uses to which experience charts can be put.

Appendix

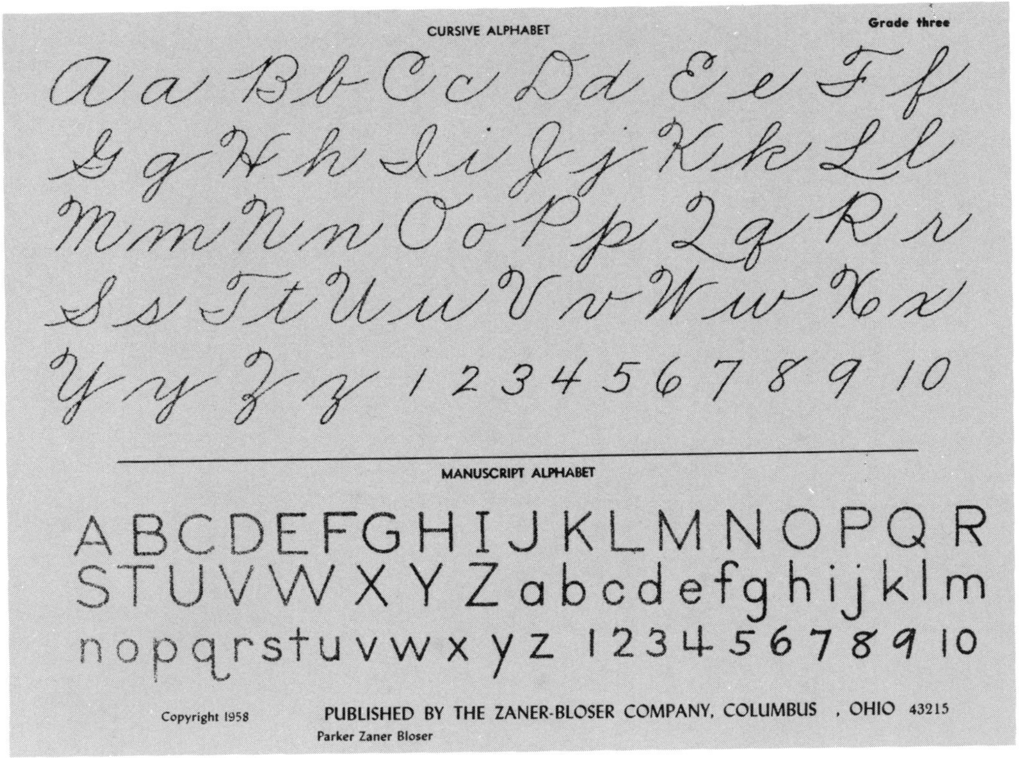
CURSIVE ALPHABET
Grade three
Aa Bb Cc Dd Ee Ff
Gg Hh Ii Jj Kk Ll
Mm Nn Oo Pp Qq Rr
Ss Tt Uu Vv Ww Xx
Yy Zz 1 2 3 4 5 6 7 8 9 10
MANUSCRIPT ALPHABET
A B C D E F G H I J K L M N O P Q R
S T U V W X Y Z a b c d e f g h i j k l m
n o p q r s t u v w x y z 1 2 3 4 5 6 7 8 9 10
Copyright 1958
PUBLISHED BY THE ZANER-BLOSER COMPANY, COLUMBUS, OHIO 43215
Parker Zaner Bloser

Grade Three Alphabets. Printed with permission of the Zaner-Bloser Company, from "Guiding Growth in Handwriting Textbooks."

Index

The body of this book is set in Caledonia, one of the most popular and versatile faces in use today. While Caledonia displays touches of both Scotch Roman and Bulmer, it is distinctively original. Harmoniously constructed, the face shows little contrast between thick and thin lines. Its bottom serifs are bracketless and meet the upright stems at sharp angles. Three other faces complete the book's design: Lydian italic is used for the chapter titles and the headings in the front and end matter; Spartan Medium, for the experience charts; and Garamont, for the title of the book.